DID YOU RECEIVE THE SPIRIT?

DID YOU RECEIVE THE SPIRIT?

SIMON TUGWELL, O.P.

DARTON, LONGMAN & TODD
London

First published in Great Britain in 1972 by
Darton, Longman & Todd Limited
85 Gloucester Road, London SW7 4SU

*Printed in Great Britain by
Western Printing Services Ltd, Bristol*

ISBN 0 232 51179 9

Imprimi Potest:
Ian Hislop, O.P., 10 December 1971

CONTENTS

Perhaps even today if we were to ask some christians whether they have received the Holy Spirit, they would answer, like the disciples St Paul met at Ephesus, 'we had not even heard that there was any such thing as the Holy Spirit'.

Leo XIII
(*Divinum illud munus*)

PREFACE

Blessed be god, who is always renewing his church by his Holy Spirit, making young again what had grown old (cf. Vatican II, *Constitution on the Church*, n. 4), yet always in such a way that he makes 'the last things' to be 'as the first things' (cf. the Letter of Barnabas, 6:13). For in Jesus Christ God has already, once and for all, given us all that he has to give us; in him 'it pleased all the fullness to dwell' (Colossians 1:19). Accordingly, it is the job of any writer 'learned in the kingdom of heaven' to 'bring forth things both new and old' (Matthew 13:52). Some people naturally incline more to what is new, and in this they are not necessarily at fault. 'Don't remember the former things, don't bother about the things of old. See, I am doing (or, making) a new thing' (Isaiah 43:18f). 'See, I am making (or, doing) all things new' (Apocalypse 21:5). Others would subscribe more readily to that other, equally scriptural, saying that 'no one who drinks old wine, wants new; "for" he says "the old is good".' (Luke 5:39). So long as neither tendency becomes absolutised, a *parti pris*, both have their place within the church. It is the one Lord, 'the same yesterday, today and forever' (Hebrews 13:8), who works all in all. In so far as we are really seeking simply his will, seeking to penetrate into the dynamism and the stillness of his everlasting purpose, to enter (as it was said of St Catherine of Siena) 'into the innermost closet of God's divine providence' and to see there 'what order was taken for things to come in the world' (*Life*, by Father Fen, Part 3, ch. 2), then we shall be able to hold together in the unity of the Spirit and in love, for all our different attitudes. And God will be glorified thereby.

The Spirit is saying many things to the churches today. It is

at times hard to discern his voice amid all the other voices—
indeed, *in* the other voices. His challenge comes to us, as often
as not, through very human and fallible channels. It is the duty
of the pastor and the theologian to attempt to 'test everything
and hold fast what is good' without 'quenching the Spirit'
(I Thessalonians 5:21 and 19). One way to do this is to try to
expose the new to the light of the old. Not, of course, simply to
match them against each other in an external, mechanical, sort
of way! But, believing that the 'tradition of the church' is, in
some way, enlivened by the Holy Spirit, that it is, in fact, the
transmission down the ages of the life given to the world in
Jesus Christ, the theologian can attempt to enter into it authentically and freely, uniting himself with the catholic church not
just in its world-wide universality, but also in its temporal
catholicity, and so sharpening the instinct of his faith, to judge
(as St Thomas Aquinas might say) what is fitting, *conveniens*, in
the things that are new.

The advice of the Chinese philosopher is still pertinent:

> Returning to one's roots is known as stillness.
> This is what is meant by returning to one's destiny.
> Returning to one's destiny is known as the constant.
> Knowledge of the constant is known as discernment.
> Woe to him who wilfully innovates
> While ignorant of the constant.
>
> (*Tao Te Ching*, XVI.
> trans. D. C. Lau, Penguin Classics)

It is in this spirit that I have tried to approach the subjects
treated in this book. They arise chiefly because of two independent, though surely related, developments in the church:
one is the rise of 'shared prayer', the other is the Pentecostal
Movement, which has by now spread through all the churches
and shows no signs of abating.

In so far as these are genuine moves of the Spirit, we may
expect them both to conform to the old prophetic word already
quoted: 'See, I am making the last things like the first.' And, in
fact, I think we shall find that this is so, probably to a far greater
extent than is generally realised even by their devotees. But the
aim is not simply to call in the 'old' to justify the 'new' (or *vice*

versa. I was flabbergasted recently to read in an American periodical, *Spiritual Life,* that 'one of the charges that has been leveled against St Teresa and especially against St John of the Cross is that they discouraged Pentecostalism'). My purpose is rather that 'old' and 'new' should shed light on each other.

I am aware, not terribly contritely, that the book is not as even and polished as it might be. This is in part due to its origins: it began as a pamphlet I wrote and circulated privately on prayer groups. This grew into a series of seven articles in *New Blackfriars* (March to September 1971. I am grateful to the Editor for permission to use this material here). As the articles progressed, I became aware of various important matters I had hardly treated at all in the earlier pamphlet. The same thing happened again, to a lesser extent, when the articles began to turn into the book.

All the translations, unless otherwise stated, are my own. On occasion, especially in quotations from scripture, I may have accidentally echoed previous translations; if I have unwittingly infringed anybody's copyright, it was done without malintent, and I am sorry.

The notes at the back of the book are simply references, with a minimum of bibliographical information. They should probably be ignored by most readers.

To satisfy the curious, I have also listed most of the people and writers quoted or mentioned, with brief notes as to who they were and when they lived. Modern authors I have generally omitted.

Finally, there are a few appendices, in which I develop some points which seem relevant and important, but which could not be fitted into the main text without obscuring the general line of thought.

I hope that this book may help somebody somewhere to feel after God and find him. If there is anything in it that turns out to be contrary to the mind of the church, I pray that it may be blotted out from the minds of all who read it.

And may Mary, the mother of the Lord, pray with us, as she did with those first disciples at Pentecost, that upon us too the Holy Spirit may be poured out, the Spirit of wisdom and revelation, that the eyes of our heart being opened, we may know the hope of our calling, and rejoice with unspeakable and holy joy, and speak with boldness the word of God. Amen.

SIMON TUGWELL, O.P.

Oxford
    October 1971.

CHAPTER ONE

PRAYING TOGETHER

PRAYER MEETINGS, shared prayer, meditation groups, this
kind of thing, under various names and guises, bids fair to
become increasingly a part of the common experience of religious people, even in circles where they were previously
unheard of. Underneath all their widely differing aims and
procedures, there is one thing they all have in common: the desire
actually to meet God, to come face to face with him, not just as
a theory or a concept, but as a living reality. People are dis-
satisfied with religion that does no more than preach and
moralise; they want the real thing. It is time we woke up to the
fact that people want more from the church than bingo and
dances: they want God.

Obviously, at its worst, this may mean no more than a crav-
ing for new experiences, for spiritual 'kicks'. But that is no
excuse for settling back comfortably into the old, lethargic
mediocrity. The idea that religious experience is only for the
privileged few, and that 'ordinary christians' (as if that were
not straight away a contradiction in terms!) should not aspire
to it, is neither traditional nor sound. 'I cannot imagine,' writes
Brother Lawrence, 'how religious persons can live satisfied
without the practice of the presence of God.'[1] And the Second
Vatican Council came up with the rather inspiring thought,
that 'the glory of God the Father in Christ is this, that the work
of God accomplished in Christ should be received by men
consciously, freely and gratefully, and shown forth in their whole
lives'.[2]

In the eastern church, it has been the monks, on the whole,
who have constantly proclaimed the need for religious experience. In the west, especially of recent centuries, it has rather

been the hallmark of certain Protestant churches, although
catholics have never been entirely silent on the subject. However, it is to the Protestants that we owe the 'prayer meeting', in
which people come together to pray in the freedom of the
Spirit, with no rules beyond the rule of Faith and Love, expecting the Lord to guide and direct the meeting, and accepting
in faith that he does so. It is only recently that Catholics have
started attending, and even holding, such meetings, and it can
be a strange, even worrying, experience for some people,
though others find it immediately exciting.

It is wholly in accord with the mind of the church, as expressed officially in the Second Vatican Council, that Catholics
should recognise and learn from the spiritual treasures found in
the Protestant churches. As the Council says, these are part of
our heritage too, and necessary for the full development and
manifestation of our own catholicity.[3] There is no reason, a
priori, why prayer meetings should not be one such treasure, to
bring joy and blessing to Catholics, as they have to so many of
our separated brethren in Christ.

It is quite extraordinarily difficult to give any satisfactory
account of what a prayer meeting is all about, because each one
is liable to be so different from any other. A healthy group,
relatively free from inhibitions and fears, goes this way and that,
free as the wind, as the Spirit guides it. And then there are all
the various human factors which come into play, all the cares
and hopes, the joys and depressions, the inhibitions and the
exhibitionism. And groups can get stuck for a time, so that you
think no one is ever going to open his mouth again (or to stop
shouting, depending on the people!). So much can go wrong,
and so vastly much more can go right, that I can hope at best
to give a very hazy impression of what is involved in a prayer
group. Please God it may stir a chord or two in those for whom,
in his providence, it is intended.

People sometimes talk as if prayer were a purely human act;
but this is not christian doctrine. Prayer is the act of the
believer, the one who says, 'I live now not I but Christ' (Galatians 2:20). It is only in Spirit and Truth that we can offer
acceptable prayer to the Father (John 4:23). It is because
Christ prays, that we, in the same Spirit, can pray. Prayer is a

divine activity in which we, by grace, participate. It is always
'the Spirit and the Bride' who pray (cf. Apocalypse 22:17). We
can only pray because God himself gives us prayer. 'I am
ground of thy beseeching,' as the Lord said to Julian of Norwich.[4] In our prayer meetings, therefore, we seek to pray with
the prayer that God himself gives us.

Now, as we become more and more sanctified, our prayer
too becomes more and more attuned to the prayer of Christ.
This is our hope and our aspiration.

But we must beware of two, antithetical, traps on the way.
On the one hand, we must not assume forthwith that anything
we utter at a prayer meeting is automatically underwritten by
God. At times, we may get a deep, irresistible, assurance that
our prayer is truly willed by God, or we may get corroboration
some other way; but that is another matter. On the other hand,
we should not sit and wait until God actually forces something
out of us. We may, perhaps, apply here too the advice Abbot
Chapman used to give: 'pray as you can, not as you can't'.[5]
We must start where we are. There may be a great gulf set
between our 'own' prayer and that of the Spirit, but both are
important. The process of christian maturing is, as the Fathers
say, the 'mixing' of our spirit with the Holy Spirit, the mixing
of the leaven of the kingdom into the lump of our human dough
(Luke 13:20f). If either ingredient is missing, the process cannot go on. It is only in so far as we offer ourselves to God as we
actually are (not as we would like to think we are, let alone as
we think we ought to be) that he has the raw material to work
on. Grace builds on nature; take away the nature, and grace
cannot build.

So we must come to prayer as we are, and let the light of
God expose all our murky thoughts and desires. The very im-
possibility of bringing them out openly before other people in
the group may well be the means by which the Holy Spirit too
convicts us inwardly. It can be a very painful process, and this
is, I think, one of the things that can drive people or keep
people away from group prayer. At times, it is as if a searchlight
were turned on the depths of the soul, not by the other people
(who may know nothing at all of what we feel within us, unless
the Lord chooses to show it to them), but by the Lord himself.

But if we let the light shine in our hearts, then even our darkest thoughts, our most sordid yearnings, will become light. It is the devil who wants them to remain hidden, just below the level of articulation. As soon as they are formulated, in the light of prayer, we can see through them, and they wilt. This is one purpose of our praying together.

Just as importantly, we also seek to accomplish the work that the Lord may have for us in prayer. It shocks our philosophical sensitivity to admit that prayer makes any difference; but the whole witness of scripture and of the saints teaches us that it does. '*Ask,* and it shall be given to you' (Matthew 7:7). Just as he does in other ways, here too God gives us a perfectly real independence. We do not *have* to pray, and if we do not pray, the work is not done.

This is obviously not simply to say that our creaturely desires influence God's will and make him change his mind; but it is worth noticing that that is, in fact, how prayer, at least the prayer of the prophet, is sometimes presented in the bible. In Exodus 32:7–14, for instance, Moses entreats the Lord, who has determined to destroy the people of Israel, and the Lord 'was sorry for the evil he had said he would do' to them. The Lord does nothing without telling his prophets (Amos 3:7), and their rôle is not simply to acquiesce, but to advise, to plead (Jeremiah 23:18; Genesis 18:16–32), to make God change his mind (Amos 7:1–6).

In similar vein, we read of the great abba Sisoes, who inherited the place where St Anthony the first hermit had lived: 'Abraham, the disciple of abba Sisoes, was once tempted by a devil. The old man (Sisoes) knew that he had fallen, so he stood up and stretched out his hands towards heaven and said, "God, whether you like it or not, I shall not leave you alone unless you heal him." And he was healed immediately.'[6] If this seems irreverent, it is no more so than our Lord's own parable about the widow and the unjust judge, which he told to encourage us to persist in prayer (Luke 18:1–8).

Of course, it is God himself who stirs his servants thus, as it were, to withstand and challenge him. He wants to be defeated. When Phinehas intercepted a God-sent plague, 'it was counted to him as righteousness' (Psalm 106:31). The Lord invited St

Catherine of Siena to 'offer holy desire and continual prayers
. . . because I want to do mercy to the world';[7] when she pre-
vails against him in prayer, he says, 'you see that you have
bound me with this bond, and it is I who gave it to you'.[8]

It is therefore *within God's will* that we must pray, in his own
Spirit and through his Son who is 'alive to make intercession' for
us (Hebrews 7:25). Our God is not a static, unchanging One,
such as philosophy knows of; he is Trinity. He is Father, source
of all being and beauty and love, origin of all things; he is Son,
eternal Will of the Father, in whom all things were made; he is
Spirit, the gift given to men, whose name is Gift, poured out
and distributed so that his very unity seems at stake, unless we
'preserve' it (Ephesians 4:3); the Spirit yearns in us for the
recapitulation of all things in Christ, when the kingdom will be
finally submitted to the Father, and God will be all and in all.
That is our God; and our prayer is part of the dynamism which
is his truth, his life.

First and fundamentally, the prayer is always: 'Come, Lord
Jesus.' The prayer of the Spirit and the Bride is always for the
coming of the kingdom. But it is for the coming of the kingdom,
not just in its perfection at the end of all things, but here and
now in particular situations, where the victory of Christ is to be
shown forth. We pray for healing, to show that Christ 'has taken
our infirmities and borne our diseases' (Matthew 8:17). We
pray for peace, that the unity of men achieved on the cross may
be manifested. We pray for a nice afternoon, that God's children may rejoice and again rejoice.

So in prayer, we ask God himself to choose and to direct our
prayer according to his will. And he does this, often in remarkable ways. We may, for instance, be just about to pray for
something, when somebody else chips in with just the words we
were going to say, even though, perhaps, naturally speaking, he
knew nothing at all of the matter that was on our heart. Or we
may be led to pray for someone we know nothing about, only
to learn later that some great work of grace has been achieved.
Again, the Lord may give an unmistakable spiritual exultation
when certain things are prayed for, that we may know that it is
according to his will that we pray for them. There are many
ways in which he moulds us and our prayer; only experience

can teach, as only experience can testify, that the Lord *does* lead prayer, and does answer it, according to and often far surpassing the measure of our faith.

In praying together, we are also led into a deep fellowship with each other. People who have never met each other before become closely united in prayer, and this often lasts and is maintained in their lives ever after. People become more than naturally sensitive to each other's situation, and sometimes one member of a group becomes quite telepathic towards another. They may even 'visit' each other in spirit, when they are apart in the flesh, and this can be known clearly to both parties. This seems to be what St Paul meant, when he writes to the Colossians, 'even if I am not there in the flesh, yet in spirit I am with you, rejoicing as I observe your good order and the firmness of your faith in Christ' (Colossians 2:5); or to the Corinthians, 'when you are assembled together and also my spirit, with the power of the Lord Jesus . . .' (I Corinthians 5:4). In this way, we can be a great support to each other in prayer, even when we are not physically together in the group.

In fact, prayer is found to be a natural and deep medium of communication. There is a real fellowship in the Holy Spirit, which becomes a known reality in prayer meetings, and overflows into the rest of our lives. A genuine, spiritual charity springs up in our hearts, that charity which is the only source for authentic christian morality, as St Thomas teaches,[9] following St Paul. Without charity, even the highest virtue is worthless, even benevolence and philanthropy are beside the point. And this charity is something quite real in its own right; it is not the same as natural attraction or goodwill, though it obviously does not contradict them. It is a supernatural faculty developed in us under the inspiration of the Holy Spirit.

It may sound from all this, that a prayer meeting is characterised by an austere—or perhaps exotic—supernatural remoteness. Just the reverse! To be supernatural is precisely the fulfilment of our nature; and as we become filled with the Holy Spirit, we become much more profoundly human, more profoundly natural. It is quite common for there to be laughter and joy, or weeping, or even shouting and clapping, at prayer meetings; this is a natural response to the way the Lord is making himself present. There may be a joy too great to contain, or a yearning which passes beyond words; there may be a sorrow which breaks one's heart. Yet in all these, there is a peace, an integrity, which will always be found to distinguish the genuine article from the hysterical or induced (emotionalist) counterfeit.

To an 'outsider' this response may seem exaggerated at times, because he cannot 'see what it is all about'. One of the things that happens, as one enters more familiarly and deeply into prayer, is that one becomes spiritually more sensitive, sensitive to things that our normal senses cannot pick up. One becomes attuned to spiritual atmosphere, one becomes a more subtle 'instrument', as the Fathers say, for the Spirit to play on. We learn to note more and more subtly the working of the divine Spirit; we develop the ability to 'hear what God has to say' (Psalm 85:9). This develops as we gain in the courage to follow 'hunches'; some of them turn out to be genuine promptings from God, others turn out not to be. If we never follow them at all, we shall never learn to distinguish them. But if we take the risk, and make mistakes, we can become wiser and more discerning.

Usually the experiential awareness of God begins as 'heat' and only later develops into 'light', as the Fathers teach. That is to say, at first one knows only a sort of diffuse warmth, of varying intensity, which indicates that the Lord is present to us. This is what the Fathers call 'the feeling of God'. It may or may not lead to an emotional response; in itself, it is very matter of fact. Any spirituality which does not lead to this kind of realistic feel for the things of God can safely be discounted. The contemplative is the one who is able to be realistic at every level—though his realism of course contradicts that of the 'man of the world' (cf. I Corinthians 2:9ff).

Later, the understanding is found to have matured in a new way, so that it moves more confidently than before in the realm of divine truth. We have growing within us 'the mind of Christ' (I Corinthians 2:10–16), and we are 'anointed' by God's own Spirit, 'so that we do not need anyone to instruct us' (I John 2:27).

This development is not necessarily easy. It may be extremely

painful, in fact. Everyone has heard of dark nights, and they are
a very real experience for those who allow God to remake them
in his own image. They may find that their whole world col-
lapses, the world which gave them meaning and security; they
feel lost and exposed. Worse, they find that what they used to
regard as their christian faith is shattered. God, in becoming
more real, becomes decidedly less tame. He 'is not a pussy cat',
as Archbishop Anthony Bloom remarks.[10]

Depending on a person's previous attachment to the world,
to his own private and tamed world, this weaning and re-
making will be more or less prolonged, more or less continuous,
more or less painful. God is taking over, and that means being
carved up by the Word of God, 'which is sharper than any two-
edged sword, actually dividing even soul and spirit' (Hebrews
4:12). It is all too easy to chicken out at this stage; but if we
remain faithful, God leads us through into a world of joy and
freedom past anything we could have conceived of before.
Because this new joy and freedom are his, they depend on
nothing transient. We have been brought through death, and
now there is nothing we need fear. There is nothing that can
separate us from the love of God in Christ Jesus.

Of course, the old Adam does not just lie down quietly and
die. There remains much in us that goes on screaming, that
goes on being afraid, concerned, anxious, recalcitrant, that often
seems to get the upper hand. But yet, after all, that turns out
not to be the last word. Deeper in us even than ourselves, there
is, there really is, this new life, even in spite of our remaining
fears and disobedience and all that; the new life goes on, the life
which is Christ himself living in our hearts by faith. As we go
on, this becomes more and more real, and so, step by painful
step, takes control over more and more of our lives, dragging us,
forcing us, into the light and freedom of the sons of God.

Increasing sensitivity to the Holy Spirit makes us also more
sensitive to other things too. As we become aware of freedom,
we become proportionately aware also of bondage. We become
aware of our moral life in a completely new light. The concern
to correct our behaviour gives way to a desire to oust all that
holds us inwardly in bondage. It is not so much our outward
acts that we tackle, as our inward 'passions', which we feel,

increasingly, to be alien, even demonic. At first this may even result in a deterioration in our behaviour; this is the price we pay for increasing awareness and honesty. Things we had previously repressed very successfully, now emerge; only so do the murky depths become exposed to the light of Christ. Obviously this is not to say that we now let every impulse have free rein! Only now that we are concerned with a much deeper level of moral awareness, we have much less energy to spare on keeping up appearances. Our behaviour, in becoming more integrated, inevitably becomes more transparent—a mixed blessing, at first, for most of us! But never mind. It is probably only our pride that suffers; other people are much more hurt by our hypocritical kindnesses than by an honest insult. Christ comes for the sinner, and the more we know, really know, experience ourselves to be sinners, the closer we can come to Christ. We give up our own attempts to be righteous, and 'await' a righteousness which he will give us in his own good time (Romans 10:3; Galatians 5:5).

However much we may suffer, it is just not worth balancing against the glory. Even now, so far from perfection as we are, such gifts are lavished upon us! There can be a joy in the Lord, which reaches down to the very depth of our souls, and reaches up in praise to the very throne of heaven. I suppose praise has not featured prominently in the spirituality of most Catholics; yet it is common in prayer meetings for a whole group to be caught up in praise, sometimes with a clear awareness of fellowship in Christ with the holy angels, whose whole life it is to praise God, and with the saints who have gone before us (cf. Hebrews 12:22ff). Similarly with thanksgiving: people experience quite unexpectedly sometimes a great gift of thanksgiving, even in acute suffering. This is a wonderful experience. It does not in any way deny the suffering, but yet you cannot, for the moment, help saying over and over again, 'Thank you' to God. And this is what St Paul told us to do: 'thank God *at all times*' (I Thessalonians 5:18).

CHAPTER TWO

THE PRINCIPLES OF
GROUP PRAYER

'How do you know it's not just hysteria? Isn't it just sheer emotionalism? Or perhaps even from the devil?' These are real questions, even if they are sometimes asked in a spirit of fear and antagonism, and they deserve a serious answer. Much of the rest of this book will, in fact, bear upon them; here I shall just outline a few essential principles.

The fully free human act is one in which every level of our being is integrated and harmonised: reason, intuition, imagination, emotions, subconscious, physical instincts, and so on; and in which we are at one with the whole environment, and in accord with the deepest nature implanted in us by God our creator.

But we are fallen, fallen from our nature, fallen into disharmony with our environment, fallen into disintegration within ourselves. The spiritual life is the gradual restoration of harmony and wholeness, by the grace of God, until we attain to the measure of the stature of the fullness of Christ (Ephesians 4:13).

It is only God, according to the scholastics,[11] who can move us from within, without in any way detracting from our freedom. 'When a man is inwardly disposed by the gifts of the Holy Spirit—and this is, in fact, a way of telling whether a man is spiritual or not—he feels himself remarkably free in all he does. unconstrained and unimpeded, without confusion, obstacles or inhibitions, for 'where the Spirit of the Lord is, there is freedom' . . . In case we might make the mistake of thinking that people born of the Spirit are being driven by some kind of raving mad urge, like those whom some evil spirit has got hold of, the first thing the Lord requires on the way of the Spirit is that he should 'blow where he wills', to show that birth from the Spirit enhances rather than destroys freedom of choice' (John of St Thomas).[12]

Any manifestation that is from God will therefore leave us entirely free—more so than we were before, in fact. It will leave us at peace, 'humble under the strong hand of God' (I Peter 5:6), and deeply tranquil. A manifestation that comes simply from a stray bit of ourselves, whether from a conscious attempt to work ourselves up, or from a dissociated bit of subconscious (as in hysteria) will give us, or at least everyone else, a feeling of strain and compulsion, and will leave us het up and awkward and very conscious of 'I' (aren't I a good mystic?). Similarly with any diabolical influence.

Humility and tranquillity cannot be counterfeited. Once you have known the real thing, according to the Fathers, you need not seriously fear delusion, provided always that you never let go of humility. Accept even the fact that you are proud, if you are, and you will have turned even your pride towards humility. For humility is simply the direct, undisguised, objective recognition of reality. Reality is God's greatest ally. So long as we simply let the facts be, whatever they are, we are in God's hands, and he will keep us from error and bewitchment. 'Let be, and know that *I* am God' (Psalm 46:11). We should cultivate a calm, detached equilibrium, 'resting' on God (cf. Psalm 37:3: *bṭaḥ*, generally translated 'trust', seems originally to mean 'to lie down flat on' something); then we shall easily learn to recognise in ourselves, or at least in each other (we can always help each other here, provided we are not too polite!) anything that is false or affected.

The Lord himself once gave us a word about this, which has been abundantly proved true. It was given at the very first meeting of a new prayer group; and the Lord simply said: 'in the stillness of your heart you will know me'. And we thank God for this.

The chief thing to be watched in a prayer meeting is 'short-circuiting'. It is all too easy to say 'Praise God!' at the top of your voice, just because everyone else is doing so. It is easy to pick up an external idiom of prayer, without really entering into prayer. It is especially easy to get carried away quite unprofitably and unprofoundly by exuberant group singing. Singing is terribly important, but it must be prayer, not an evasion or a substitute for prayer.

We should learn a deep inner silence, so that anything we say, or sing, or shout, comes from deep down. As deep as we can manage (though, once again, 'pray as you can, not as you can't'). That will not make it infallible, but it will mean that our prayer is always reaching deeper and deeper down, till eventually it will be really rooted in God's own will.

If we find ourselves praying in an assumed or unnatural voice (it can happen), we should beware. If we find ourselves thinking, 'Why isn't anything happening? I must try and stir things up!', we should beware. One thing we can be quite sure of: anything that is not fully *our* prayer, will not be God's prayer either.

So much for the dangers, at any rate for the time being. But what are we to say now on the positive side? What does it really mean for us to come together to pray with each other? Is it simply because we enjoy doing so, or is there something deeper and more important than that? (Not that enjoyment is an inferior or insignificant motive! Would that all christians enjoyed prayer more!)

The basic principle of group prayer is the teaching of our Lord, that 'where two or three are gathered together in my name, there am I in the midst' (Matthew 18:20), and that 'if two of you agree about anything on earth in prayer, it shall be granted' (ibid. 18:19).

We are together the Body of Christ, and as such 'members of one another' (Ephesians 4:25). As christians, we belong together, and it is natural and proper that we should exercise together our most specifically christian privilege of prayer.

And conversely, prayer should be the most natural thing in the world for christians to engage in when they meet. After all, as christians, we can no longer meet simply as man to man: what holds us together, and makes it possible for us to meet at all, is the Spirit of Jesus Christ himself. And he who unites us to each other, is he who also unites us to God, and is indeed God himself.

When St Clare came down to Santa Maria degli Angeli to have supper with St Francis, before they could turn their attention to the meal, the whole company was caught up into such a brilliance of contemplation that the neighbours thought the place was on fire![13] And it is just as true today that the Lord will visit his people with his wonderful presence, in so far as we allow ourselves to be open to his coming.

'Do not get drunk with wine, but be full in spirit, speaking to each other in psalms and hymns and spiritual songs, singing and making music to the Lord with all your heart, giving thanks always and for everything and everyone in the name of our Lord Jesus Christ to God the Father!' (Ephesians 5:18-20.) That is St Paul's idea of a party!

It is, then, perfectly natural for christians to pray with each other. But it is also our duty. From the very beginning, the church has rebuked those who would separate themselves from the fellowship of prayer. St Ignatius the Martyr writes to the Ephesians: 'try to meet more often to give thanks and glory to God. When you are often together, the powers of Satan are thrown down.'[14]

Originally it seems that there was no distinction made between praying together formally and liturgically, and informal spontaneous group prayer. Even the Eucharistic Prayer, the Canon of the Mass, was originally extemporised;[15] and it seems probable that the whole assembly would have taken part in various ways (except perhaps the women—see I Corinthians 14:34. St Paul is very probably thinking only of the particular situation in Corinth).

Times have changed, and it would be fruitless to speculate about the likelihood or desirability of our ever returning to the simplicity and freedom of the early church. We do have to make the distinction between set prayer and spontaneous prayer; though woe betide us if we try to play one off against the other!

There should be no need here to explain at length the importance of liturgical group prayer, where the church acts in her official capacity, praying with all her divinely given authority in the name of Jesus her Head. Here, in the words of the church, we do indeed know that the Spirit himself intercedes for the saints according to the will of God.

But it is of the nature of the case that such formal prayer should be general; it cannot and should not provide for the particular and specific needs of any given time and place. The attempt to make liturgy always topical is fundamentally misconceived. It is of the essence of the liturgy that it should be 'routine' prayer. And we *need* this; this is our prayer-world, the framework within which we can learn to live the life of christian joy and freedom. Our prayer does not originate with us, it is a cosmic process, it is a divine process, initiated by God himself; we are invited to take part in it, but it is not primordially 'our' prayer. We relax, we settle down into an ongoing process of prayer, we let it subtly and gently mould and sustain us. We do not—or should not—expect it to be always a great 'experience', any more than we expect our morning cornflakes to be a great 'experience'. But if we are deprived of it, we notice it. Of course, this is not to say that we shall never see the glory or the light in the liturgy; probably our highest experiences of prayer will come in the liturgy—the Mass is, after all, the very centre of our christian life. But these peak experiences are not, strictly, what liturgy is about; it is not designed to give us an 'experience'. The most wonderful thing about it, is that it is simply *there*. It is a kind of prayer we can just 'slip into', which, in a sense, requires very little deliberate effort of us. We attend to it as best we can, but it does not depend upon our effort. We can participate quite properly even when we feel exhausted and unable to concentrate. And we do need this kind of prayer. Those who complain that the new liturgy does not meet this need, have a perfectly valid complaint, though perhaps it is not really the new rite as such that is to blame.

In addition to this kind of prayer, though, the church has always recognised the importance of 'private' prayer, and, in general, has acknowledged that even when a person prays alone, his prayer is never in the strictest sense 'private'. It is always the church at prayer; one cannot pray at all, except in the fellowship of believers, not to mention the angels and the saints. This prayer is our personal dialogue with the Father, through Jesus Christ and in his Holy Spirit; just as the glory of each saint in heaven is different from every other, so even here the divine calling of each one of us is peculiarly his own. And this not just in general, but in each particular moment of his life. This is why it is not enough to follow the general rules, the moral principles: life is not lived in the abstract, but in the particular. The rules, the laws, the principles, are the roadsigns the white lines down the middle of the road, the traffic lights and No Entry signs; they define an area within which we can drive. But the actual driving requires far more than just that! It requires a particular and specific response to each particular situation.

Similarly our lives in Christ require each moment a particular, specific response to the will of God in Christ. According to St Thomas Aquinas,[16] the new law, the law of the Spirit of life, is not a set of external rules and regulations, not a new spiritual Highway Code, but the actual indwelling of the Holy Spirit. The traditional teaching of the church is that, in addition to the virtues (which are our obedience to the general principles of moral behaviour), we need the gifts of the Spirit, by which we are made docile to the particular leading of God in specific situations. These gifts are said to be actually necessary for salvation.[17]

And God's leading is not something impersonal; it is always, or can be, a personal encounter with him in Jesus Christ. This is part of the meaning of the injunction to 'pray always, without intermission' (Luke 18:1; I Thessalonians 5:17). Our prayer, at its most basic level, is our dialogue with God in faith and obedience to the particular way in which he is making himself present to us at the given moment.

And here, too, as in every other aspect of our christian lives, 'no man is an island'. It is very natural and proper that christians should pray not just individually, but also in groups, in twos and threes, with Christ in the midst, listening to the will of God, and seeking to pray the prayers that God himself puts into our hearts.

Whether in liturgical or in free prayer, it is always 'the Spirit and the Bride' who pray; the Bride prays because the Spirit gives her prayer. In the liturgy, the public, official prayer of the church, we simply accept, in faith, that here the Spirit is at work, that the prayers given to us and spoken in the name of the whole church are truly according to the will of God.

In our informal meetings for prayer, we have no such external guarantee. We must therefore, seek to be led inwardly by the Spirit, to pray the prayers that God desires of us. And, as I have already said, it is the experience of many groups that this leading does come. God *does* place prayers in our hearts and on our lips.

CHAPTER THREE

CONTEMPLATION AND CHARISM

WE MUST NOW TURN our attention to a convergence that is becoming apparent, between what I am saying about prayer meetings, and the traditional teaching about contemplation. God-given, or 'infused' prayer is generally regarded as the hallmark of contemplation, and that, one might think, is something far removed from prayer meetings!

Let us not judge over-hastily, and, above all, let us not simply pit against each other two stereotypes, and declare them incompatible. There is more to the contemplative than appears in sentimental pictures of nuns rapt in silent ecstasy, just as there is more to a prayer meeting than a gathering of fanatics who cannot stop talking. In each case what is surely central is the claim to be experiencing God, to be entering into God-given prayer, to being directly aware of the truths proclaimed by our religion.

In strict theological terms—here I follow de la Taille's helpful little pamphlet, *Contemplative Prayer*[18]—the contemplative, although he may *feel* that he has received a totally new gift of grace (and, in one sense, obviously *has*), nevertheless he is really only coming to experience what has always been with him since his baptism. *All* true prayer is 'infused'; the contemplative knows it by experience. The beginning of contemplation is, in scholastic terms, the conscious coming into play of the gifts of the Spirit bestowed in principle at baptism, but only now beginning to exercise their proper rôle in actual life and experience.

And this is precisely what is experienced by many people in prayer meetings. The grace of God breaks through to them, and they begin to *know* what they had always professed to believe, or perhaps, in some cases, had even stopped believing, but knew they were supposed to believe. What are we to make of this?

The Carmelite school of mystical theology has rather led us to think that the dawn of contemplation is something that simply 'happens' to us. We should no more pray for it to come, than the child should pray to wake up six inches taller! (Though by the by, it would be a funny child who did not aspire to grow.)

But the older teaching, including that of St Thomas, is not quite so passive. The origin of all christian teaching about contemplation, as such, is monastic; the monks, in face of a world becoming superficially christian, developed practices designed to help them preserve the fullness of the christian faith and hope. At their best, they fairly consciously avoided passing judgement on those who remained 'in the world'; but, for their own purposes, they taught that, until their 'Renunciation', or 'Conversion' in St Benedict's sense, they had lived as if still subject to the law of sin and death, under the law like the old Israel. At their 'conversion' they were delivered from the law, and entered the freedom of the new law, the law of the Spirit; they were freed from servile fear, and came under the domain of love. This, clearly, developed into the regular teaching about the ages of the spiritual life, beginning with servile fear, from which one is freed by love which casts out fear (which St Catherine explicitly connects with the experience of Pentecost, [19] which transformed the apostles from men afraid, into men aglow with love and boldness and freedom of speech before men and God).

On this view, it is, in quite a real sense, up to us to decide to stay at the level of law and fear, or to move on to the level of love and freedom. Up to us, because to move on is quite simply to claim the promise made to all christians. The monks never thought they were doing more than simply being christians; their question was always, 'How am I to be saved?' And what they experienced was surely but the fuller operation of baptismal grace. What it is all about, is simply entering into the inheritance of all christians.

The monks effected this entry by making some decisive move, a move *away* from the world, and all its cares and concerns, its worries and its desires, its ambitions and its responsibilities (thus making visible and effective in living experience the baptismal renunciation of the pomps of Satan), and a decisive move *towards* a kind of life which professed, and, at least to some extent, embodied total dependence on and adherence to Christ. This could and did take extremely diverse forms; but in every case there was a real step to be taken, a bridge to be crossed, a boat to be burned. One did not become perfect overnight; but one did enter a 'state' of perfection.

Theologically, we must never lose sight of the total dependence of the contemplative life on the sacraments: baptism is its beginning, communion its daily bread. But psychologically we can see that taking some decisive step of the kind we have been considering can place us in the way of *experiencing* the grace received implicitly in the sacraments.

And a step taken, to some extent, publicly, is all the more potent. This is why, long before religious orders were invented and given canonical status, one did not become a monk privately. There was always some kind of group with which one professed to involve himself; at the very least, it took one other person to make you a monk.

Now, you do not have to be a monk to be a contemplative. But it does seem that it can be helpful for there to be some kind of step which one can take, to make manifest his determination to let Christ have more of his life, and, indeed, all of it. Although there can be no question of repeating the objective grace given once and for all at baptism, some such step can help us towards the full experience of our initiation in the Holy Spirit, which is, after all, the birthright of every christian.

So, in prayer groups, it is commonly the case that, at some stage, people come to a critical point, a 'point of no return'. This may just happen, suddenly and unsolicited; the grace of God sometimes goes straight to work on us, entirely ignoring the censor in our heads. Or God may work more slowly, and people can sometimes find that something has happened to them, they have been changed, though they could not say exactly when. Otherwise, and perhaps this is the most frequent case, the Lord waits to be asked, stirring our minds and our hearts to *seek* the breakthrough, the experience of grace.

In such cases, it is often helpful for the group to pray for a person, that he may receive some clear token of God's real presence in him, some unmistakable 'introduction' to the Holy Spirit, which will at least begin to drive out fear, a touch of God's finger which he can never quite go back on, and which will, if he goes with it, lead him into ever more subtle recognition of God's promptings, setting him on the way (no more, obviously!) of love and freedom and boldness before God and men.

The gesture of laying on of hands is a traditional and convenient one to use on such occasions. It is a sign of blessing, and does not necessarily connote any official, sacramental authority on the part of the people concerned. It helps to focus our prayer for one another; and we should not be ashamed to allow our bodies their proper share in our spiritual lives. It has certainly been the experience of many people that this simple, fraternal gesture can add immense power to a prayer, and will often win down a blessing that had previously been sought in vain.

One reason why this prayer of the group can be so helpful is that 'God resists the proud, but gives grace to the humble' (James 4:6): there is a degree of humility involved in admitting one's need before men, and asking them to pray for one, that of itself will dispose us to receive the grace that is offered.

Also, we know that the Lord looks, not only on our own personal faith, but also on that of the church, and of particular church fellowships. In Matthew 9 we read how some people brought a friend of theirs who was paralysed to Jesus; Matthew tells us that it was in response to *their* faith that the man was healed and his sins forgiven (Matthew 9:2).

In fact, it is evident that we can at times minister Christ to others to a far greater degree than we are conscious of his presence to ourselves. Like the widow who, because of her obedience, found herself giving Elijah far more than she actually had (I Kings 17:8–16), we too can minister Christ to others, by his grace, far in advance of our own union with him. Have we not all, at some time or another, found ourselves giving advice, or whatever it might be, far wiser than we ourselves knew? These are little signs that Christ is indeed at work through us, as well as in us.

The church has always taught that we must distinguish between God's work *in* us and his work *through* us. The former is what sanctifies us, the latter is for the good of others, though, if we are open, we ourselves will receive a grace on the rebound, as it were. It has been the consistent teaching of the church that even dramatic examples of God working *through* us are no indication of our own degree of sanctity. A prophecy can be given through Balaam's ass, if need be!

Now, on the one hand, this is a warning against pride: the fact that the Lord can and does use us, does not necessarily even mean that we are in a state of grace. But on the other hand, it is an encouragement to our humility: we do not have to wait till we are saints before we can minister Christ, even in dramatic ways, to each other.

In a group, then, we can all minister Christ to each other, to a degree far surpassing the individual sanctity of any one of us in the group. Thus we can build up the church in the power of grace, we can pray and praise God in his own Spirit and power, and in so doing advance the sanctification of each one of us.

We may call this the 'charismatic' aspect of group prayer, in that 'charism' has come to be restricted, in common usage, to this area of graces given for others through us, And, in so far as we allow and expect it to happen, our meetings may well be led by God into the various charismatic manifestations (prophecy, healings, tongues, interpretation, etc.), all of which, as we well know, have characterised the lives of many of our canonised saints, but which could and should have much wider scope in the church. The saint is, after all, simply the fully-fledged, normal christian. We are *all* called to be saints, as the Vatican Council reminded us;[20] and we become saints only by allowing the grace of God free play.

This always means that, in one sense, we will be 'playing at' being that bit holier than we are; for God, according to St Cyril of Jerusalem, is 'he who makes the play-actor into a true believer'.[21] In the Mass, *par excellence*, we 'pretend' to be perfect and in so pretending, become that bit more perfect; in acting as if we really were the church without spot or wrinkle, we gradually become more like that.

In fact, we must always seek to 'lift' ourselves up above ourselves', as the Lord exhorted St Catherine.[22] In a group we can help each other to do so. And it is likely that, in one form or another, our real point of spiritual breakthrough will come when we find ourselves doing something that we could not possibly be doing. This sometimes takes the form of the gift of tongues, which is (to say no more for the present) a simple and harmless gesture from the Lord on our behalf, a way of empowering us to act beyond our own natural capacity, ministering grace charismatically, though in this case chiefly to ourselves (for he who speaks in tongues 'builds himself up'— I Corinthians 14:4). Or it may be something quite natural in itself, but which we had always regarded as quite impossible for *us*—it might be weeping, for instance, or lifting up our hands and shouting, 'Praise God!'. The Lord has many ways, and is as devious to us as we are to him (Psalm 18:27). However it comes to us, this is the point where faith begins really to come alive, and our lives to be turned inside out.

CHAPTER FOUR

CATHOLICS AND PENTECOSTALS

I T IS CHIEFLY to the Pentecostals that our century owes the existence of charismatic prayer groups, and it was they who recovered, on a significant scale, the practice of laying hands on people for the blessing of the Spirit, and expecting something—generally the gift of tongues—to happen. What began as an unwanted revival within North American evangelical Protestantism rapidly became one of the most flourishing religious movements of the century, and now comprises within itself several denominations of its own (for instance, the Elim churches, and the Assemblies of God); it has also infiltrated back into the older churches, including, most recently, the Roman Catholic.[23]

Since 1967 there has been a growing Catholic Pentecostal Movement in North America. It began as largely a lay movement, in Catholic university circles in the U.S.A. It received massive and sensational publicity, and grew with amazing speed, spreading throughout the States and penetrating into Canada. In 1969 it received cautious approval from the U.S. hierarchy; it has also been more enthusiastically recommended by one or two individual bishops.

Although it is a very variegated phenomenon, running right through it there is the insistence that all christians can and should claim 'the promise of the Father' in what they, with other Pentecostals, call 'baptism in the Holy Spirit'. That is to say, people who are already believers in Christ call down upon themselves or, more generally, upon each other, an outpouring of the Holy Spirit, 'just as it was in the beginning' at Pentecost. The usual procedure is for someone who has already had the experience to lay hands on one who is seeking it, and to pray for him; it is believed that this will result, by God's gift, in a sudden or gradual unfolding of the person's life in Christ into the charismatic manifestations, usually beginning with tongues, followed in due course by prophecy, interpretation, healing, or some such supernatural endowment or ministry. It is claimed that a great many people, some on the point of leaving the church or the priesthood altogether, have found their christian lives amazingly invigorated and renewed; they have entered a new freedom in prayer and witness and action, a new joy in the Lord, a new love for God and man; in many cases also an increased devotion to the sacraments, and to our Lady, and, of course, very close fellowship with christians of other denominations who have also shared in the Pentecostal experience.

Now, the question 'What's happened to the Holy Spirit?' is not a new one in the church. Leo XIII, in his encyclical *Divinum illud munus* of 1897 lamented that some catholics seemed hardly even to know of the existence of the Spirit.[24] And one of the great controversies of the earlier part of the twentieth century was whether the mystical and charismatic way was, in principle, proper for all christians; the Dominican Garrigou-Lagrange[25] and the Jesuit de la Taille[26] argued strongly that it was, the other side being represented most weightily by the Jesuit Poulain, whose *Graces of Interior Prayer*[27] remains an outstanding monument of the purely phenomenological approach to mysticism. The Benedictine Anselm Stolz, exhorting us to return to a more ancient, patristic, theology, showed that the question should never even have arisen.[28] Then, in more popular vein, Bede Jarrett[29] and Gerald Vann[30] both drew our attention back to the Holy Spirit, to the reality and efficacy of his presence in us. J. G. Arintero (1860–1928, perhaps the greatest spiritual director and writer of the period, and one of the leading figures in the revival of mystical theology) taught insistently that all christians not only *could*, but *should* aspire to the highest mystical union with God. And he warned against the tendency to fight shy of the charismatic gifts.[31]

More recently, Karl Rahner has laboriously reminded us of the patent intention of St Ignatius in his *Spiritual Exercises* to lead people to a direct experience of divine guidance, and of the spiritual and theological importance of this.[32]

Then, to crown it all, Pope John had us all praying to the Spirit to renew his wonders in this our age 'as by a new Pentecost'.[33]

But, for all the preaching and teaching, the discussion remained largely academic. The question what to *do* about it remained unanswered, perhaps inevitably in view of the prevalent belief that mystical prayer must not be actively sought, but would simply 'come' in God's good time. There was some excellent and practical teaching on prayer—the simplicity of Vincent McNabb's *The Craft of Prayer*,[34] for instance, is highly commendable—but it all served to make contemplation seem even more remote and unlikely. A great gulf seemed to be set between 'ordinary' prayer and 'mystical' prayer; there seemed no way through for the majority of christians.

Into this situation, the Catholic Pentecostal Movement clearly comes as a major breakthrough. Its emphasis is practical in the extreme—'Pentecostalism is not a theology, but an experience', they like to say;[35] it offers easy access, to all and sundry, into spiritual prayer. And it manifestly 'works': things do actually happen to people. Things actually happened to me, things have happened to people I know well.

However, there are problems, and in matters of the Spirit it is dangerous to confuse naïveté with simplicity. We must be fools for Christ, and simple as doves; but we must also be cunning as serpents (Matthew 10:16). John Wesley gave as his second advice to those caught up in spiritual renewal: 'Beware of that daughter of pride, enthusiasm. Oh, keep at the utmost distance from it! . . . You are in danger of enthusiasm every hour, if you depart ever so little from scripture; yea, or from the plain, literal meaning of any text, taken in connection with the context; and so you are, if you despise, or lightly esteem, reason, knowledge, or human learning; every one of which is an excellent gift of God, and may serve the noblest purposes.'[36]

Theology, like sin, cannot simply be disposed of by denying it. While doing full justice to the experiential vitality of Pentecostalism, we must 'keep our cool' and recognise that it also—inevitably—carries with it a theology, which must be scrutinised carefully in the light of sound exegesis of scripture, and theological learning.

There is, after all, no such thing as pure 'experience', devoid of all context. The world we live in, our upbringing, values, associates, state of health, all kinds of factors, considerably affect the way we experience things, and conversely, our experience inevitably affects our view of things. In religion, there is a complex dialectical relationship between scripture, personal experience, and the context of our church fellowship, theological studies, and so on. This is a perfectly healthy process, and it is one of the ways in which the Holy Spirit leads the church into all truth, and this is, at the deepest level, what is meant by church tradition: it is the living mediation of the deposit of faith given once and for all, by the operation of the Holy Spirit.

When the Tradition is healthy, it communicates a wholeness of personal and corporate experience, an understanding of and familiarity with scripture, not as dead words from the past, but as a kind of living language, and a mature and developing christian culture and wisdom. Unfortunately, we are all more or less victims of a fragmented, and often moribund, tradition. Spirituality and dogma have parted company, and theology has tended to shrink to a handful of isolated and rigid slogans, generally survivors from long forgotten, once real, controversies. Until recently, catholic exegesis was proportionately sterile, bearing fruit, if at all, largely by way of sentimental misapplication of texts.

A 'tradition' in this unsupple state is singularly vulnerable to 'enthusiasm'; because it is both stiff and full of holes, it is liable at times both to swallow and to reject more than it should do.

In Ezekiel's vision of the valley of dry bones, the promised renewal consists of both a reassembling of all the scattered bones, 'bone to its bone', and a new inbreathing of the spirit of life (Ezekiel 37:7 and 9ff).

So it must be with us. In the long run, we shall do God better service, we shall advance his work in the world more faithfully (if less spectacularly), if we attend not only to the exciting new breathing of the Holy Spirit, but also to the relatively humdrum job of reintegrating all the bits and pieces of our fragmented tradition, and our lost wholeness.

When it comes to Pentecostalism, this seems to be especially problematic. On the one hand, there are the pro-Pentecostal books, which stand firmly on experience, but with little serious attempt to cope with the various theological and exegetical issues involved. Their use of scripture is often rigid and tendentious. On the other hand, there is the anti-Pentecostal literature (see most recently Dr J. G. Dunn: *Baptism in the Holy Spirit*[37] and Professor Frederick Dale Bruner: *Theology of the Holy Spirit*[38]), which presents an overwhelming theological and exegetical case against them, but hardly begins to do justice to their evident spiritual vitality.

What is necessary, and what I hope to attempt here, is a thorough scriptural and theological enquiry, which is open both to the data of revelation and tradition *and* to the spiritual experience of Pentecostalism. If at times this seems pedantic and devious, nevertheless I believe the exercise is worth undertaking and may, indeed, be vital for the authentic renewal of christian life in the church.

CHAPTER FIVE

'HE WILL BAPTISE YOU IN THE HOLY SPIRIT'

'BAPTISM IN THE SPIRIT' is the most distinctive and controverted doctrine of Pentecostalism; it was the hallmark of the original Pentecostal movement, and it still is the hallmark of all Pentecostal-inspired renewal in all the churches, including now the Roman Catholic.

Essentially, the doctrine is this: after conversion (and 'water baptism'), there remains a second blesisng, associated usually with the laying on of hands, in which one receives the 'fullness' of the Holy Spirit, and his personal indwelling, experiencing for oneself what the first disciples experienced at Pentecost. Some manifestation, usually tongues, is generally expected; indeed, strict Pentecostals demand it—'no tongues, no baptism in the Spirit'. Thereafter a person should increasingly realise in his life that he has been 'endued with power from on high', power to witness for Christ, he will know that he is 'led by the Spirit', he will expect to receive and, when necessary, to perform miracles, especially healing. Appeal is made to texts like Mark 16:17f, and the obvious passages in Acts—all the texts that respectable commentators like St John Chrysostom have had to explain away.

I have no desire to devalue the experience referred to by the Pentecostals. But, if we are fully to appreciate its significance, both for our theology and for our spiritual development, I think we must subject it to a thorough and patient scrutiny in the light of the whole teaching of scripture and the tradition of the church, and so try to determine its precise spiritual and psychological meaning. Later we shall also have to say something about the gift of tongues.

The gospel begins with the appearance of St John the Baptist, preaching a baptism of repentance in view of the impending arrival of the Messiah, who is to execute an eschatological baptism of judgement in Spirit and fire. The New Testament shows us both how Jesus does fulfil this expectation, and how, importantly, he does not. Even after the Resurrection the apostles are still thinking in terms of a dramatic and violent dénouement (Acts 1:6); they are still thinking within the same categories as the Baptist. Then suddenly, at Pentecost, there they are proclaiming that, in spite of the complete lack of violent or dramatic demonstration of messianic power, as it had generally been understood, yet Jesus *is* the Messiah, the judgement has taken place, complete with the eschatological baptism, in the form of 'this which you see and hear'—a crowd of people noisily praising God in 'other tongues'. Therefore 'be baptised, and you too will receive the Holy Spirit' (cf. Acts 2:38).

An important step in all the gospels is the baptism of Jesus. According to the Baptist's prophecy, Jesus would be the one who would baptise. Instead, he comes to be baptised—the whole thing is upside down (Matthew 3:14). There was an early Jewish Christian tradition that actually located here the baptism in Spirit and fire: as Jesus went down into the waters, 'there was fire kindled in the Jordan'. This fire is clearly the fire of judgement, and Jesus is said to 'escape' from it; his escape is followed immediately by the descent of the Spirit and the proclamation of his Sonship.[39] There are echoes of this in the canonical gospels (for instance, Luke 12:49f). Jesus' messiahship is exercised, not in the execution of the baptism of judgement, but in submitting to it. We can see in the New Testament how the Baptist's prophecy about him baptising, although retained, is not followed through (notice especially John 4:1f, which betrays a real embarrassment at the mention of Jesus baptising. In Acts 1:5, it is significant that Jesus says simply, 'you will be baptised', not 'I shall baptise you in the Holy Spirit', as one would expect from the Baptist's prophecy).

Jesus does not undergo baptism simply in our stead. He is baptised in our midst (cf. Luke 3:21) and we are to share in it with him (Matthew 10:38). His messiahship is shown precisely in that he, having passed through the waters of death and been raised up to receive the Spirit (Acts 2:33), pours him out upon those who believe in him.

Not that we should separate their belief from their reception of the Holy Spirit. In Acts 11:17 St Peter seems to date the apostles' own belief from Pentecost. We must remember that the position of the first disciples was quite unique: they were the company of those who attended Jesus in his whole earthly ministry (Acts 1:21f). At Pentecost they finally and decisively enter into fellowship with him in his exaltation, which is the culmination of his ministry, by the reception of the Holy Spirit. What thereafter is achieved all at once in the sacrament of baptism, in which a man mystically dies with Christ and is raised up with him even to the right hand of God, is, in the case of the first believers, spelled out over their years' living with Jesus. We may recall the sacramental principle, that in the sacraments we are united with Jesus *as he really is*. Therefore, argues St Thomas, if there had been a consecrated host reserved at the time of Christ's death, we should have to say that he died also in the reserved host. It is the same Christ in the sacrament as on the cross.[40] Before the exaltation of Jesus there could be no real christian baptism, because, in St John's extraordinarily bold language (diluted in almost all translations) 'as yet there was no Holy Spirit, because Jesus had not yet been glorified' (John 7:39).

The Jews who passed, with Moses, through the sea and the cloud, could be said to have been 'baptised into Moses' (I Corinthians 10:2); similarly the reality of christian baptism, baptism into Christ, is that we pass through the sea of death with him, entering into the cloud with him, so that there may be found 'only Jesus '(Luke 9:34–6).

This explains why the apostles, after their reception of the Holy Spirit at Pentecost, which sets the final seal upon their own long association with Jesus, go straight out to invite men to be baptised, with the promise that they too will receive the Holy Spirit.

We should notice that Luke's Pentecost story is exactly correlated with the exaltation scene at the end of Matthew, and the appended conclusion to Mark's gospel. The exaltation of

Jesus, the believing of the disciples, their experience of the Holy Spirit, and the preaching of the gospel and baptism are all inseparably bound up together.

This is further substantiated in the case of St Paul. He had not known the Lord at all in the flesh. What Pentecost was for the other apostles, baptism was for him, as his letters bear eloquent testimony.

Apart from Pentecost itself, the only other passage in Acts which refers to anyone being 'baptised in the Spirit' (and that only indirectly) is in the story of Cornelius. Here, as at Pentecost, the Spirit appears to fall independently of baptism. Pentecost, as we saw, was a unique situation, concerning only those who had lived with the Lord in the flesh; its extension to others takes place by way of baptism. And in fact the culmination and point of the Cornelius story too is the reception of him and his household to baptism; the Holy Spirit comes down manifestly upon them all, it seems, to force Peter's hand in allowing gentiles to be baptised. This was what God was showing them that he wanted, and who was Peter to refuse him (Acts 11:17)?

It looks as if St Luke knew that he had to do something with the Baptist's prophecy; having seen it safely through into christian baptism, first for Jews, then for gentiles, he can let it slip.

It is surely quite in keeping with this pattern in scripture that the church has always applied the texts about baptising in the Spirit to the sacrament of baptism. And I think we must face squarely the fact that catholic theology is, frankly, more or less exactly opposite to Pentecostal theology on this point. For Pentecostals, water baptism is a human act attesting our faith in God, while the second blessing is the work of God alone. For us, the sacrament of baptism is the work of God alone, and as such a pure and perfect work, while the second blessing (or any subsequent religious experience), however blessed and momentous, is a work of co-operation between God and man, a stage in the process of man's divinisation by the Spirit of God, a part of that 'mixing' of the leaven into the human lump.

We may quote St Augustine as a typical spokesman for the catholic view. Basing himself on John 1:33, he says that baptising in the Spirit is a work reserved incommunicably to Christ alone. There is one Lord, one baptism. Therefore, whoever baptises, it is the Lord who does it: 'whether Peter or Paul or Judas, it is He who baptises',[41] using the minister (as St Thomas will add) simply as an instrument.[42]

As the great Byzantine scholar, Nicholas Cabasilas, argues, baptism is a perfect and complete work, because of the complete perfection of the work of Calvary. If, therefore, the grace seems to be received in varying degrees, let us not blame the sacrament, but rather the recipient.[43]

I think this can easily be misunderstood, where the full, traditional teaching about the sacraments has got lost. There has been a tendency in western christianity to make a sharp separation between God's act and man's (if it's me, it isn't God, and vice versa). The older theology, including that of St Thomas, sees that any divine act in our lives is always also a human act. 'The Spirit bears witness *with our spirit*' (Romans 8:16). This is why we are bidden to be somewhat reserved in face of any religious experience of our own, however overwhelming; it will always be an experience of God *and us*. It is only in the human life of Jesus that there is a pure manifestation of God; it is in his dying and rising again that our redemption is, objectively, wrought. And this objective redemption is made available to us, quite objectively, in the sacraments of the church; in them, as it were, that humanity in which God is perfectly manifested is extended down the ages. Where the rite is properly performed, there, by divine ordinance beyond anything we can control or defile, there is a perfect act of Christ. By contrast, any experience of our own depends upon our spiritual state. Catholic theology therefore reserves to the sacraments the absolute faith that here there is a pure and perfect work of God, and denies this theological weight to any other religious manifestation.

'The kingdom of heaven is like a man scattering seed upon the ground; he goes to sleep, he gets up again, night and day, and the seed sprouts and grows, he doesn't know how. The earth produces of itself, first the blade, then the ear, then the full grain' (Mark 4:26–8). The seed can grow even without our knowledge. If a sacrament is an act of God in Christ, a *real* act, then it does its work even if we feel nothing—provided we are not blocking it.

However, this is not to say that experience does not matter. If we read the New Testament, doesn't it rather suggest that all christians are (not 'should be'; *are*) characterised by a kind of spiritual *experience*, an experience of being set free from Law and fear and sin and even sickness and death; an experience of being set free from themselves? They apparently knew what St Paul was on about when he appealed to them, 'Was it by works of the Law that you received the Spirit?' (Galatians 3:2); or when St John talked of the way in which we 'know' everything because of the 'anointing' we receive from God (I John 2:20); 'in this we *know* that he dwells in us, from the Spirit which he gave us' (ibid. 3:24).

There is no reason to suppose that the early christians were all that much more virtuous than most of us, the evidence is against it. But yet, they do seem to have known in their own experience the reality of the victory of Jesus Christ, the reality of the indwelling of God, of the Spirit who explores even the hidden things of God (I Corinthians 2:10). By virtue of their baptism, they seem to be given access to this whole world, a world we can only call 'contemplative', in that it rests, not simply on blind dutiful obedience to the precepts and teaching of the magisterium, but also on experience. (It goes without saying, that they knew nothing of the modern tendency to oppose doctrine and mystical experience.)

Nor is this confined to the first generation. There is a little piece by a certain Jerome the Greek, who appears to be a monk; we do not know when he lived. He answers the question, 'How do you know you were baptised at all? Perhaps your parents were secretly pagans.' 'I know it,' he replies, 'from the results. Isaiah says, "through fear of you, Lord, we conceived, we were in travail, and we gave birth to a Spirit of salvation" (Isaiah 26:18 LXX), showing that we who have been enlightened through baptism have received the Holy Spirit. Elsewhere God says, through the prophet, about those who are baptised, "I will dwell in them and (literally) walk about in them" and "I will pour out of my Spirit upon all flesh". All who have received the divine Spirit in themselves (literally, in their womb) in holy baptism, are assured inwardly in their own heart that they have indeed been baptised, by the leapings and prickings of his grace, by exultations and workings, by his, so to speak, jumping up and down in them. . . . A pregnant woman feels the baby stirring inside her; so they know from the joy that is in them and the happiness and exultation in their heart, that the Spirit of God dwells within them, whom they received in baptism . . . a pregnant woman doesn't have to be *told* that she is pregnant, she knows it from the facts . . . similarly it is not by hearsay, by the assurance of his parents who had him baptised, that the true christian should seek confidence that he did indeed receive holy baptism; he should be assured in no other way than by his own heart.' Jerome claims to be speaking for 'lots of people in the world' (i.e. not to mention monks).[44]

The early christians were not especially more virtuous than we are; yet in one sense, their position was different. They had all, in a much more positive sense than most of us, renounced the world. They had not, of course, geographically separated themselves; they did not constitute a ghetto. Far from it. But they had detached themselves from the ambitions and hopes of the world, from its satisfactions and desires, from the 'language of the world', as St John of Ávila calls it[45]—they did not allow the world to determine their understanding of life, they did not look for the meaning of things in the common assumptions and prejudices of men. They had left behind them the security of simply belonging to their age, being 'men of their time'. They had, in however small a degree, become the 'bearers of essentially different needs, goals and satisfactions' (Fergus Kerr, O.P., paraphrasing Herbert Marcuse).[46] They had let Christ actually transform them; they had abandoned the world of darkness, in favour of the wonderful light of Christ.

The total picture that emerges can perhaps be resumed under the one word, conversion, *metanoia*, which, as St Luke especially brings out, is both the prerequisite for entry into the Kingdom, and itself the first fruit of the Kingdom. Quite literally, it is the 'new heart' which is implanted in us by the Spirit, which is, indeed, from one point of view, actually the Spirit himself indwelling us (Ezekiel 36:26f); it is 'the mind of Christ' (I Corinthians 2:16). Baptism does not, certainly, *consist* of a spiritual experience, but it involves a man, clearly, in a whole new dimension of experience. From the very earliest days of the church, it contained, at least tacitly, a definitive renunciation of Satan, a dropping-out (*apotaxis*) from the ranks of the Prince of this world and all his pomps (including the mystical ones— for 'the devil hath his contemplatives', as the *Cloud of Unknowing* warns us).[47] It includes the confession of faith that 'Jesus is Lord and Christ', and this confession is embodied in one's life by a real abdication of care (this is a great theme of St Matthew's), whether care to justify oneself (that is now Christ's business), or care to look after one's interests in the world, or even care to defend one's reputation and property.

Although it is often convenient to distinguish between the work of grace by which we personally are saved, and that by which we are endued with charismatic gifts, ultimately we must recognise that there is only the one reality, which is the mystery of Christ, the economy of God's redeeming plan for mankind. In baptism we are caught up into this whole divine economy, the whole reality of Christ. Whether we manifest this in the moral transformation of our lives, in contemplative wisdom, in supernatural prayer, or in the working of miracles, in all these it is the same Spirit, the same Lord, working all in all. We cannot pick and choose. 'He who does not gather with me, is scattering' (Matthew 12:30). In the last analysis, there is no room for partitions and categories; Christ is not divided, and our life in him is fundamentally but Christ himself living his own life in us.

In the New Testament, in the early church, all that Pentecostals understand by 'baptism in the Spirit' is referred quite strictly and simply to what it means to be a christian at all. The experience of the Spirit is not subsequent to that of conversion and faith; the experience of Pentecost is identical with the baptismal confession that 'Jesus is Lord' (and how often the New Testament warns us against Pentecostal manifestations divorced from this confession!).

Unfortunately, we have to recognise that, generally, our own experience of baptism, of being christians, falls far short of this wholeness, this integrity. The Pentecostal doctrine is intended to be one way of coping with this situation, by allowing an

independent reality to conversion, and to the experience of the
Spirit in his fullness.

But perhaps this is too easy a way out. Our enquiry so far
has driven us back to fundamentals. What is at stake is the very
reality of our christian initiation, our baptism, what it is to be a
believer at all. Pentecostal talk can easily obscure the real issue,
I think; it strikes people as exotic, it appears to set up two
classes of christians on a highly tendentious basis, its exegesis is
idiosyncratic and, in general, unconvincing by the standards of
modern scholarship or traditional theology. All this makes it
too easy to evade the problem. The whole thing looks rather
different when we are driven back, as we seem to have been, to
the single reality of the life of Christ in us. It throws a very
direct challenge to those who are content to have been validly
baptised, without aspiring to supernatural awareness or to a
ministry and witness in the power of the Spirit, indeed without
expecting to be 'changed' (in the pregnant sense common to
Symeon the New Theologian in the east and Wesley in the
west), those, in fact, who only know 'from hearsay' that they
have been baptised at all.

On the other hand, there is a salutary reminder also for those
who do aspire to the experience of the Spirit. The New Testament warns us that there can be Pentecostal phenomena
(phenomena 'in Spirit') that are not from God, that are not
part of the mystery of his will in Christ. Where only part of
Pentecostalism (that which concerns the 'baptism in the
Spirit') has been adopted, as by many renewal movements in
the historic churches, the necessary safeguards easily get lost.
There can be a Pentecostal experience without any real commitment of faith, without the basic determination that Jesus
Christ is to be the interpretative context for anything that happens. There can be an 'experience of the Spirit' that is not an
experience of the exalted Christ, that neither issues from nor
into *metanoia* (and, I repeat, *metanoia* cannot be deliberately
produced, it is itself the first fruit of the Spirit; it is not that a
man *says* he has committed himself to Christ. It somehow
shows). There should be no question of seeking something *extra*,
something other than the basic reality of the salvation wrought
in Christ, and our incorporation into Christ in baptism. There

are no 'perks', there must be no looking for 'experiences', only a desire to see the work of Christ made real in us and through us. This must, of course, include experience; if our lives are truly being changed, they will feel different, and the range of our experiences will shift. But what we are seeking is God's will in Christ.

'Do not rejoice that the spirits are subject to you; but rejoice that your names are written in heaven' (Luke 10:20).

CHAPTER SIX

THE MANIFESTATION OF BAPTISM

IN THE LAST CHAPTER, we tried to grasp something of the full New Testament understanding of baptism, of what it is to be reborn 'of water and the Spirit'. We saw that it should be, and indeed, so far as the evidence shows, really was a spiritual turning point, leading a person into a whole new world of experience and truth, with its own canons of under-standing and behaviour, its own distinctive principles of action, both moral and charismatic. We saw that there was an in-dissoluble complex of: faith in the exalted Christ, *metanoia* (conversion, having a new heart), renunciation of Satan the Prince of this world (dropping out, *apotaxis*), the experience of the Spirit of God 'who explores even the hidden things of God', who 'convicts the world', who leads us 'into all truth'.

We had to admit, however, that not many of us experienced our baptism that way. Somewhere along the line, baptism (con-version) and the experience of the Spirit seem to have parted company. How can we face this all-too evident fact, without betraying the equally evident teaching of the New Testament?

Already in the New Testament we find some important guide-lines. For instance, there is a very significant shift between Matthew and Mark.

For Matthew, faith is a key concept, closely tied to his pre-sentation of the exaltation of Jesus, to whom all power in heaven and on earth is given. The question Jesus asks is, 'Do you believe that I can do this?' (9:28). The answer must be simply and totally, 'Yes, Lord', an answer that entails a radical abandonment of care, a total upheaval of the normal procedures of social life (which is what the sermon on the mount adds up to).

Mark, by contrast, introduces a process of growth, a time lag. Mark alone develops the parables of growth (4:26–32). For Mark the life of the church issues, not from a sudden and glorious Pentecost or a triumphant Exaltation scene, but from an empty tomb and a few frightened women (it seems to be generally agreed now that 16:9–20, which are not contained in the best manuscripts, are not part of the original gospel— though this does not mean, of course, that they are not part of inspired scripture). For Mark, the christian is the one whose faith grows: 'Lord, I believe, help my unbelief' (9:24). There can be a gradual healing (8:22–25), miracles do not necessarily come all at once (11:12–14 and 20–24). When we pray, we are to believe that we *have* received what we ask for, and it *shall* be ours.

Paul, as we might expect, has it both ways. For him, the christian life is strung between 'you have been saved' and 'you are being saved'. 'By hope we were saved', he writes to the Romans, using the past tense; 'by grace you have been saved', to the Ephesians, using the perfect tense. But 'to us who are being saved', using the present participle in I Corinthians 1:18 and again in I Corinthians 15:2 and II Corinthians 2:15. In Christ 'you are dead': therefore 'do to death your members that are upon the earth' (Colossians 3:3f).

Everything is rooted in the once for all death of Jesus, in whom we too die once for all in baptism; we have put on Christ, the Spirit has revealed to us 'what eye has not seen and ear has not heard'. Yet the experiential realisation of what has been given may not mature all at once. Each one of us must live up to whatever degree of realisation he has reached (Philippians 3:16) and, like Paul himself, press on, forgetting what lies behind and stretching out towards what lies ahead.

The paradox comes out most acutely in the Letter to the Ephesians. In Christ we have been called and made holy and blameless before God, even before the foundation of the world (1:4). By his sheer grace, at our baptism we were sealed with the Holy Spirit, and made alive with Christ; we received the enlightenment (one traditional name for baptism) which made us know the 'economy of the mystery which was hidden from all ages in God who made all things' (3:9; cf. 1:9). Yet the

writer prays 'that the God of our Lord Jesus Christ, the Father
of glory, may give you a spirit of wisdom and revelation, in
the knowledge of himself, that the eyes of your heart being
enlightened, you may know what is the hope of your calling,
what is the wealth of the glory of his inheritance in the saints,
and what is the surpassing greatness of his power in us who
believe, according to the exercise of the might of his strength in
raising Christ from the dead' (1:17–20).

This is no invitation to spiritual laissez-faire! The New Testament is highly critical of a faith that refuses to mature. 'By this
time you ought to be teachers, but instead you need someone to
teach you all over again the first principles of God's will'
(Hebrews 5:12). We should not shelter too cosily behind the
principle of growth. The gardener is patient, but in the end he
will ask whether our baptism has borne fruit—and 'fruit' must
not be confused with 'works': we can, by an effort of will, 'put
our religion into practice', but that does not necessarily mean a
thing.

Why is it that so often our baptism shows so little sign of
bearing fruit? What has gone wrong, and what are we to do
about it?

One answer is, basically, moralistic. 'They have indeed the
form of holy baptism, but none of the light, for they have been
deprived of the light by a cloud of sin.' That is the answer given
by St Catherine of Siena. Our baptism is dead, because, when
we came to years of discretion, we did not obey the laws of God,
and so did not enter into the experience of light, but rather
'blew it out with a wind of pride', leaving ourselves blinded by
'the cloud of self-love'.[48] If this is our condition, we must repent
and make a good confession, and reform our ways.

A parallel solution is adopted in the east by Symeon the New
Theologian, one of the greatest of Byzantine monastic re-
formers, and a great preacher of mystical prayer. With him it
leads to a detailed and exciting theology of *metanoia* (which he
occasionally calls 'baptism of the Spirit', in fact), and I should
like to spend some time on this.

In his Catechetical Lectures, St Cyril of Jerusalem had
warned his catechumens that 'if you persist in any evil purpose,
the water will receive you, but not the Spirit'.[49] In similar vein,

Symeon maintains that a baptism without genuine conversion is a baptism only in water. It is only the 'second baptism', that 'of the Spirit', which actually makes one a real christian and a child of God, and this is brought about by *metanoia*, manifested in tears (he calls it a 'baptism of tears').[50]

In spite of terminological similarity, it is clear that Symeon is much closer to Wesley than to the Pentecostals; and his position is open to the same objections. His concern for spiritual efficacy leads him seriously to under-rate sacramental objectivity (he does this in connection with ordination and confession too, though his doctrine of the eucharist is objective and realist in the extreme).[51] He leaves himself wide open to the charge of mystical subjectivism, as his critics and enemies were quick to point out.

However, if we discount this, making the necessary allowances, I think we shall find that he has much to teach us.

Symeon's whole theology is based on his own experience. When he was still a layman, without any of the normal ascetic 'qualifications', he was led into profound mystical experience of light by his spiritual Father, Symeon the Studite. Subsequently, if we can believe his own account, he all but lapsed from the faith, and was only reclaimed, once again, by his spiritual father, to whose prayers he thereafter ascribed all his rich spiritual and mystical experience.[52] Even more than most Greeks, he insists on the rôle of the 'intermediary', the 'friend of God' who procures favours, all undeserved, for his disciples. (See Appendix III for an elaboration of this point in connection with prayer groups.)

In Symeon's view, the man in bondage to sin lies by the wayside, 'mentally paralysed', a gruesome sight for those with eyes to see, unable even 'to go to the doctor' for himself. He can only hope that some 'kind physician' will come his way, some intermediary and friend of God, to make peace between him and God. For Symeon there can be no question of a man working up *metanoia* for himself; he is utterly helpless.[53]

If he is lucky enough to meet up with some friend of God, he must trust him and obey him implicitly. 'And if he bids you stay in quietness, saying, "Sit here without going out, until you are clothed with power from on high", obey him with firm hope and insatiable joy. Such a teacher is true, and no deceiver. There will come down upon you too, even in this age, the same power of the all-holy Spirit, not visibly in the form of fire, but you will see it spiritually in the form of spiritual light, with all tranquillity and enjoyment . . . then every compulsive (passion-ed) thought and desire will disappear, every passion of the soul is driven off, every bodily disease is healed. Then the eyes of your heart are cleansed, and receive the promise of the Beati-tudes. Then, as in a mirror, the soul sees even its smallest faults and sinks to the depths of humility, and, appreciating the greatness of this glory, is filled with all joy and happiness, and, in amazement at this wonder which passes all expectation, tears well up from your eyes. And thus a man is totally changed and knows God as he is first known by him.'[54]

It is clear from parallel passages that this is what Symeon means by *metanoia*. This it is that leads a man from darkness into light, and not to desire the light is tantamount to refusing conversion—and Symeon gives short shrift to those who would reduce this light to mere intellectual knowledge. Such men don't know what our redemption is all about.[55]

Symeon keeps reiterating the Saviour's words, ' "Repent (*metanoeite*) for the kingdom of heaven has come close!" It has come close, it is standing at the gates of your heart and mouth. Open your heart by faith and at once it will come in, and immediately your mouth will open and you will shout out, "We've got the treasure of the Spirit in us, we have! We've got eternal life in our hearts!"'[56]

And this is not just for our private sanctification (though 'those who have not received the light have not received grace'):[57] 'the grace of the all-holy Spirit seeks to kindle our souls, so that he may shine out to men in the world, and direct the steps of many by means of those in whom he shines, so that they too may walk well and come close to the fire, and, one by one, all, if possible, may be kindled and shine like gods in our midst'.[58]

Symeon was not alone in regarding tears as the necessary sign of spiritual realisation, though he was more extreme than most. Centuries earlier, Isaac the Syrian insisted also that it is only 'when you come to the place of tears' that 'you can know that you have set foot on the way of the new age'. And he specifies that it must be uncontrollable weeping, not just an odd tear or two such as anyone can wring from their eyes.[59]

This is, in some ways, a clear parallel to the western doctrine of the prayer of quiet, in which our minds are forcibly stopped from their normal discursive thinking, and become intoxicated with the sweetness of the Lord.[60] This is the point at which Christ is actively asserting his grace in us; we are no longer in charge. And, of course, this is pretty fundamental. One of the distinguishing marks of christian baptism, as against Jewish, was that you did not do it to yourself; it is something *done to us*, we have to let ourselves go down under.

And this requires faith. Isaac, following St Matthew, sees faith as the crucial issue. For him, the point of breakthrough comes when you really launch out in faith, casting all your cares upon the Lord, 'exchanging your prudence for his providence'. We should aspire to the measure of faith, in which we become fools that we may be wise. 'Ask God that you may attain to this measure of faith; pray for it eagerly until you get it . . . then you will know beyond doubt, by your own experience, the might of him who is with you.'[61]

It also requires humility, and here let me quote a pleasant little tale from the *Fioretti* of St Francis. 'One day when the first companions of St Francis were come together to talk of God, one of them related: "there was a man, who was a great friend of God, and he had great grace both in deed and in contemplation; he also had such abounding and profound humility, that he thought himself one of the worst of sinners. This humility kept him in grace and holiness, and made him continually grow in virtue and in God's gifts, and never let him fall into sin." Brother Masseo, hearing such wonderful things of humility, and realising that it is a treasure of eternal life, began to be so inflamed with love and desire for this virtue of humility, that he lifted up his face to heaven with great fervour, and vowed with great determination never to be happy again in this world, until he should feel this virtue perfectly in his soul. . . . After Brother Masseo had been some days in this desire, it happened one day that he went into the wood, and was going about, in great fervour of spirit, weeping and sighing, asking

God with burning desire to give him this virtue. And because God willingly hears the prayers of those who are humble and contrite, while Brother Masseo was going along like this, there came a voice from heaven, calling him twice: "Brother Masseo! Brother Masseo!" He knew in spirit that it was the voice of Christ, and replied: "My Lord, my Lord!" And Christ said to him, "What are you prepared to give for this grace you are asking for?" Brother Masseo replied, "My Lord, this is what I am ready to give: I'll give the eyes in my head." Christ said, "And I want you to have both the grace and your eyes." With this the voice went away; and Brother Masseo was left so full of the grace of humility, as he had desired, and of the light of God, that from then on he lived always in jubilee; and often, when he prayed, he made a jubilee like the cooing of a dove, "U U U", and thus, with radiant face and joyful heart, he abode always in contemplation. And, having become humble, he always considered himself the least of all men in the world.

'Once, when Brother James of Falerone asked him why he never changed his tune in his jubilee, he replied happily that, when one thing contains all good in itself, there is no need to change your tune. To the praise of Christ. Amen.'[62]

We have come a long way from the simple moralistic view that it is only sin that obscures our baptism. All the passages I have cited are concerned, not just with 'morality', but with profound psychological processes and upheavals. What we are up against, as we seek to enter more fully into our christian heritage, is often not sin so much as psychological blockages and mental hang-ups, and what St Catherine calls 'the long cord of custom' in which we get tied up 'by the unlustiness of our hearts'.[63] (The Greeks, of course, generally view sin too in these terms, and perhaps in this they are wiser than we.) What is required is a transformation at a level inaccessible to reason and deliberation alone.

And I think we can discern a common pattern in all the diverse texts I have used: in each there is a readiness to let something happen to us, to take the risk of making a fool of ourselves, or perhaps, better, letting ourselves be made fools of. In each, too, there is some bodily manifestation that does not make any particularly obvious sense at the rational level (one can sympathise with Brother James of Falerone!). In each case, the mind has to let go of its prim little clutch on life, and let the body and the Spirit conspire against it—only so does a renewing of the mind also take place.

At the heyday of hesychast theology, the problem was explicitly diagnosed as how to get one's religion 'out of the head',[64] which seems a fair enough statement of our own predicament today (which is probably why hesychast texts are in such demand).

They also had another premiss, which is theologically unimpeachable, that 'everyone who has been validly baptised, has received all grace hiddenly' (Mark the Hermit).[65] The problem, then, is how to get out of the head, and identify and unite with this grace given 'hiddenly' in baptism. The aim of all their techniques of prayer and posture was to draw the mind (*nous*, the faculty of direct intuition) out of the head, into the heart, there to discover the working of the Spirit. They call this 'prayer of the heart', and by this they intend both a reference to the physical organ (this is prayer of the body, not of the reason; they tell us to pray to Jesus 'without thoughts'), and to Christ's indwelling in our hearts by faith. It is the 'manifestation of baptism'.

It is an open question how far the hesychasts drew on sources deriving ultimately from non-christian oriental mysticism. It is at least clear that they arrived at a technique, like those of the Far East, designed to quieten the superficial mind, so that, gradually, one can find a new centre of awareness, a new equilibrium, in which conscious and unconscious, mind and body, are drawn into harmony.

The rôle of the subconscious in the spiritual life would be a subject to fill several large volumes by itself; I cannot go fully into it here. But one thing is clear: we shall get nowhere, if we refuse to face up to the subconscious. A negative attitude to the subconscious leaves us prey to all kinds of unconscious motivation, compulsive behaviour patterns and so on, and carries with it, as a result, a great fear, a fear of letting go, a fear of letting anything happen to us. But if we are to get beyond a purely external morality and conventional religion, we have to face up to all these compulsions, and tackle them at the root.

Greeks and Latins converge here in a rather unexpected way. The Greeks teach us to work and pray towards *apatheia,* a state of freedom from all passions, all compulsive behaviour patterns. The fruit of this, as Evagrius says, is love.[66]

Almost exactly parallel is St Catherine of Siena's teaching about the coming of love as the first real breakthrough in the spiritual life. Self-love holds us bound, she says, in servile fear, a 'wickid cowardis dread', as the Middle English version says,[67] and prevents us from facing up to our state as it really is, and so from seeking or receiving grace for any amendment. The only remedy against this 'cowardis dread' is love, which is closely associated in St Catherine's thought with 'patience'; and by 'patience' she means something very close to the *apatheia* of the Greeks.

On either theory, we have to take the risk of letting the subconscious play its part. But, as christians, we can believe that if we do so, we shall find that in fact the seed of the kingdom has already been sown there, and that the Holy Spirit is already at work there. So we can afford to 'let go' and know that *God* is God (Psalm 46:11, literally translated) and, by co-operating with the subconscious, in grace, we shall arrive at an equilibrium in which we are centred, not just on some psychic centre in ourselves, but on Jesus Christ himself. 'God becomes our *hegemonikon*' (that which makes us tick, literally our 'controller', a Stoic term for what the Hebrews called man's heart), as St Gregory Palamas says.[68]

We are encouraged to turn aside from thinking and visualising and planning, and sink down to the deeper level of the heart, there to let God's Spirit work in us, bringing us face to face with the reality of Christ in us, the reality and power of God's will for us and for the world in him. And then prayer becomes 'like a fire of gladness springing up from the heart' (St Gregory of Sinai's description of the prayer of 'beginners'). And this prayer is truly 'the working of faith, or rather the immediacy of faith, the manifestation of baptism, the pledge of the Holy Spirit, the exultation of Jesus . . . it is God working all in all.[69]

CHAPTER SEVEN

PROPHECY AND THE GIFT OF TONGUES

IN BAPTISM we died with Christ, and all grace, in principle, and 'hiddenly', was given to us. But, alas, much can happen to thwart this total gift of grace; the 'manifestation' of our baptism is something that may take time, that may cost us much, and we should pray towards it zealously. And, as we have seen, there comes a time, at least in some people's lives, when the light of grace breaks through, dramatically and suddenly, into experience and visibility.

We have seen some of the ingredients: faith, abandonment of care, readiness to let go and be made a fool of; humility, compunction and tears, getting religion 'out of the head into the heart'. But is there, perhaps, something else, something just as vital, which we have tended to overlook?

'If you have faith,' St Cyril of Jerusalem tells his catechumens, 'you will not only receive remission of your sins, you will also do things beyond the power of men, and, please God, you will receive the gift of prophecy.'[70]

In his book, *Visions and Prophecies* (which is, unfortunately, almost exclusively concerned with visions) Karl Rahner laments that 'it can be said with but little exaggeration that the history of mystical theology is a history of the theological devaluation of the prophetic element in favour of non-prophetic, "pure", infused contemplation'.[71] Surely he has put his finger on something fairly basic here.

For Judaism of the time of our Lord, the Spirit was, almost to the exclusion of all else, the prophetic Spirit; and the text chosen to interpret Pentecost is that from Joel about the eschatological outpouring of the Spirit of prophecy upon all flesh. So precisely is this what Luke wants to emphasise, it seems, that he actually adds an extra reference to prophecy to the original text of Joel. This is at last the realisation of Moses' wish, 'would that all the people were prophets' (Numbers 11:29). In Jesus the Prophet we are a prophetic people. Matthew is quite explicit about this (5:12: 'for so they perse-cuted those prophets who were before you'. The implication is quite unambiguous in the Greek, that those he is addressing are also prophets). We are those to whom 'it has been given to know the mysteries of the kingdom' (Matthew 13:11). Like Moses, to whom God spoke as a man speaks with his friend (Exodus 33:11), we are those whom God, in Christ, calls 'no longer servants, but friends, because all that I have heard from my Father, I have made known to you' (John 15:15).

If these texts are to speak to us, I think we must give heed to Rahner's point. Our spirituality has for a very long time been heavily conditioned by a mystical theology centred on God's eternal being, in one form or another. Some writers have even encouraged us to leave behind all consideration of the Incarnate Christ, let alone prayer of petition. Vincent McNabb was quite right to denounce this as 'almost blasphemous'.[72] (It is interest-ing that scholars are reminding us, incidentally, that prayer of petition, and especially intercession, is a prophetic function,[73] to be exercised only by those endowed with the divine Spirit. 'He is a prophet and will pray for you' (Genesis 20:7).)

By contrast, the mystical knowledge that the New Testament knows of, is knowledge of the 'mystery of God's will', that is to say, of 'the economy of the fullness of the times', the plan God had in Christ from the beginning for the salvation of men and the recapitulation of all things in Christ, the breaking down the wall of separation between Jew and gentile, male and female, slave and free. At one stroke, we are compelled to see that the object of contemplative knowledge is incarnational (to do with God's action in the world) and Trinitarian (the will of God *is* Christ, and his plan, as Irenaeus puts it, is 'produced' down the ages by the Holy Spirit).[74]

And this knowledge is not simply speculative, it is highly practical. As St Thomas says of the gift of wisdom (which, for him, is the supernatural principle of contemplation), 'it directs human acts in accordance with divine principles'.[75] To know the mystery of God's will includes the knowledge of what he is doing in me for my own salvation, and through me for the good of men. And this carries with it both promise and precept; it involves me in the whole unfolding of his plan in time, which is the life of the church.

And God's eternal plan does not come to us all at once. It is 'administered' to us, according to a divine 'economy' (Ephesians 1:10). It is therefore an integral part of our knowledge to know where we have got to, individually and in general. And clearly the coming of Christ, his passion and glorification, have introduced a new and decisive element into the situation. Prophetic, contemplative knowledge must be decisively different before and after the 'coming of faith'. It is a sufficient test of a prophetic spirit to note whether or not it confesses the Lordship of Jesus Christ and his coming in the flesh.

Before Christ, prophetic knowledge was directed to his future coming. Now, though there still remains a hope for the future, and therefore there is still prophecy which points ahead, this is based on what has already, definitively, come to pass. Henceforth the basis of all contemplation, all prophecy, is the faith that Jesus is Lord and Christ, and the *metanoia*, the new life, made possible by this fact.

Therefore, just as now our prayer to God is made in the name of Jesus, in whom already all things are ours (I Corinthians 3:21), and is accordingly prayer with thanksgiving (Philippians 4:6), so all prophecy is, first and foremost, the proclamation of what God has done in Christ, it is praise of his mighty deeds.

This is the explanation of an apparent *non sequitur* in St Luke's account of Pentecost. At first sight, it is unclear how the text from Joel, so confidently brought forward by Peter, actually serves to explain the curious goings on in the upper room. One hundred and twenty people had suddenly started shouting their heads off in 'other tongues', making such a noise, apparently, that a huge crowd gathered, and was amazed to hear them all declaring the 'mighty deeds of God' in all the different languages. Tongues, clearly, and praise; but where is the prophecy? In fact, as I have tried to show, praise is, in this eschatological age, itself a prophetic function.

It is, in fact, still very much a *prophetic* function. It is in *metanoia*, in the coming of faith, that the exaltation of Jesus, the fulfilment of the Father's promise, is made manifest. And this 'the world neither sees nor knows' (John 14:17). It is we who have received, not the spirit of the world, but the Spirit of God, who 'know what we have been given by God' (I Corinthians 2:12). This makes us, inevitably, unintelligible to the world (ibid. 14; John 15:19), and we can expect to be persecuted by it, like the prophets who came before us. 'But do not be afraid: I have overcome the world' (John 16:33—'and this is the victory which has overcome the world, your faith', I John 5:4). We are not accountable to the world, as St Paul, with incredible audacity, argues: 'For "Who has known the mind of the Lord and will constrain him?"; well, *we* have the mind of Christ' (I Corinthians 2:15f, the implication being, clearly, that therefore no one can constrain *us*). 'The wind blows wherever it likes . . . so it is with everyone who is born of the Spirit' (John 3:8). The prophet, and that should mean us, is not bound by the world's canons of propriety and intelligibility. Reversing the text from John, we might say, 'we have believed, therefore we do not and cannot accept glory from men' (John 5:44; this is a key text in St John of Ávila's argument about the 'language of the world', in which words are intended, not to carry any objective meaning, but simply to prop up the conventions and ambitions and prejudices of society).[76]

This is the kind of person who can praise, because this is the kind of person who really knows that the victory has been won, and whose 'hope', therefore, 'does not let us down, because the love of God has been poured out in our hearts through the Holy Spirit' (Romans 5:5).

Praise, then, is a prophetic function, in these last days; it is also (recalling what I said about overcoming the various psychological and mental blockages preventing the full manifestation of baptism) a sign that we have indeed begun to enter into the freedom of the sons of God, that we have reached the point of the 'coming of faith', that *metanoia* has become a reality for us.

And, of course, this comes round full circle! The outpouring of the prophetic Spirit at Pentecost was first manifested, as we saw, in praise ('Shout for joy, you heavens, for the Lord has done it!'—Isaiah 44:23). But this outpouring of the Spirit is itself the fulfilment of God's promise (Acts 1:4). It is in the transformation of their own lives that the disciples know that 'the Lord has done it'. As always, the prophet is called not just to speak, but also to *be* a sign for the people. It is 'in the church' that God is glorified (Ephesians 3:21), because the church is the manifestation that he 'has done it'. 'In this is my Father glorified, that you should bear much fruit and be my disciples' (John 15:8). As St Irenaeus has it, *gloria Dei vivens homo*: 'man alive is the glory of God'.[77] It is in submitting to the coming of faith, to *metanoia*, that the disciple manifests the glory of God, and attests that Jesus is Lord and Christ.

And it is at least appropriate that the first manifestation of this should be the gift of tongues. For 'he who speaks in tongues, speaks mysteries in Spirit' (I Corinthians 14:2), and this is a prophetic function, even if not normally, without interpretation, a public one ('he who speaks in tongues, speaks to God', ibid.). Also, as many people have experienced, tongues is a gift of praise, and is often, in fact, a person's first real introduction to praise.

Further, to return to the idea of the manifestation of baptism, it provides an excellent way of pinpointing the moment of spiritual breakthrough, parallel to tears, or the prayer of quiet, or Brother Masseo's reception of humility. In this way, it can focus one's spiritual desire, and one's openness to growth in the Lord, and can provide a useful way of specifying one's prayer for grace to break through into consciousness. You cannot pray in tongues, unless you are prepared to make a fool of yourself, and let something happen to you, over which your mind has none of its usual control. You cannot engineer tongues, any more than you could engineer the kind of weeping that Isaac or Symeon was talking about, or St Teresa's prayer of quiet.

Nor should we be too perturbed by the apparent unintelligibility of it. Tongues is a gift for our own upbuilding (I Corinthians 14:4); and perhaps we might see our growth in Christ as the gradual permeation of more and more of our being by the divine life implanted in us at our baptism. At any given moment, there will be much in us as yet untouched, or only partially touched, much that is still 'world', and therefore unable to appreciate, let alone evaluate, the working of the Holy Spirit in us. We should indeed hope for a 'renewing of our minds', but first we must 'present our bodies' as a living sacrifice to God (Romans 12:1f). In tongues, we surrender one little bit of our body to him. And that should not be the end of the story. 'I want you all to speak in tongues, but much more that you should prophesy . . . let him who speaks in tongues, pray that he may interpret' (I Corinthians 14:5 and 13). As the Greek Fathers would say, first comes heat, and only then light.

Of course, there should be no question of anyone claiming that tongues is the only way into genuine contemplation, even prophetic contemplation. But it is one way of giving body to that step of faith which both attests and initiates the experience of the Spirit, and it is, in fact, if we may believe St Luke's account, the way in which the Holy Spirit first manifested himself in the church. As the first part of prophecy, with which it has always been linked, it is, at least, a suitable way into the supernatural life: it specifies a quite definite and unmistakable supernatural act, to which one can, in prayer, aspire, and it is an act which involves faith, humility, the spiritual and psychological courage to 'let go', all of which, as we have seen, are essential elements in any spiritual growth. And it involves a positive attitude to the non-rational in us (both the bodily and the subconscious), in a way that is exposed to exceptionally few hazards. I am told that Jung regarded the reception of tongues as a hopeful sign in his patients; even from a psychological point of view, it makes possible a gradual harmonisation of conscious and subconscious mind and body.

It should also lead to the natural growth of the psychic faculties which are usually repressed (this being, according to St Athanasius, a normal and proper development in any genuine spiritual life),[78] but under the pressure of the Spirit, rather than from any morbid interest in the occult for its own sake. The importance of this in an age which is so obsessed with the occult should be obvious.

In fact, it can and should ultimately lead to a human wholeness, in which one is entirely open, at every level, to be used and led by God, with no subconscious blockages or distortions.

But the chief thing about it is simply that it is a gift of God, given to us to help us to praise him. Let us not forget this! It is a gift of praise and thanksgiving, and these are the hallmark of the messianic age in which we live. It is interesting to notice how often St Paul bids us 'be thankful'; and according to Isaac the Syrian, thanksgiving is the gateway to all God's gifts and graces.[79] As the old collect said, 'in giving thanks for the gifts we have received, may we receive greater blessings'.[80]

CHAPTER EIGHT

SPEAKING IN TONGUES

I T IS ONLY in this century that the gift of tongues has come dramatically into the limelight, and, though of all the gifts of the Spirit it is the least open to serious abuse, it has nevertheless been more misunderstood and even resented than all the rest together.

However, it is not a new, let alone a Pentecostal, invention. It seems a truism to say it, but it is often forgotten, that St Paul spoke in tongues (I Corinthians 14:18). As it is essentially a gift for private prayer, there is no way of telling to what extent it subsequently disappeared from the church. There are one or two hints in the Desert Fathers, that may be interpreted as meaning tongues, as, for instance, when 'he heard Ephraim speaking as it were a well bubbling out of his mouth, all in good order, and he knew that what came through the lips of Ephraim was from the Holy Spirit';[81] and there is a passage in the *Nine Ways of Prayer of St Dominic* that could indicate that on one occasion he was remembered as having prayed in tongues; he was heard praying aloud, and everyone saw *how* he prayed, and the result of his prayer (the raising of a young man from the dead), but, uniquely, no one could recall *what* he prayed. The author labours this point, and it seems to be important to him.[82]

In addition, many catholics have long been familiar with a kind of substitute for tongues, in the use of Latin. As so often, I think our enemies can help us to see the truth, when they refer to our use of Latin as 'praying in unknown tongues'. It is interesting too to notice how many of those who most regretted the passing of Latin were people who do not understand a word of it! This should not be an occasion for mockery, it is an indication that there is in people a spiritual need at times to pray in an unknown language. In her beautiful book on the rosary, *The Rose Garden Game*, Eithne Wilkins describes the old crones praying in Rome: 'it was indeed a mumbling of beads and a praying in gibberish, a blend of Latin with Italian that such old Roman women make their own'.[83] Long before the Maharishi came along with his mantras (which are meant to be unintelligible to the person using them), the catholic church was praying and meditating in this way.

And there are occasional unambiguous indications of people praying quite specifically in unknown tongues. The great seventeenth-century Benedictine, Father Augustine Baker, describes in his *Confessions* how he received the gift of tongues (not that he knew what it was, but it is unmistakable).[84] And there is clear evidence that the Curé d'Ars prayed in tongues.[85] There is no occasion for catholics who receive the gift today to feel that they are strangers in the house.

So, what exactly *is* speaking in tongues? It is that one speaks words which do not mean anything in any language known to himself. It is not ecstatic in the strict sense (some modern translations of the bible are misleading here); the speaker retains full consciousness throughout, his mind being alert and sober (though perhaps exhilarated). It remains his choice whether to speak or to stop speaking, though he may sometimes feel obliged to speak, in the familiar sense of the expression. And, of course, the compulsive speaker may find that he is on to a good thing!

Sometimes a person's first experience of tongues just comes to him out of the blue; at first he may not even realise what he is doing. But thereafter and normally one decides for himself to start speaking in tongues. In no case is there any suggestion of being 'taken over'. This is what distinguishes it from any hysterical or mediumistic phenomenon. One of the criteria the early church evolved, in fact, for judging true prophecy, was that the prophet should retain his normal consciousness throughout.[86] As I have already said, God's action in us makes us more free, more ourselves, more integrated than we were before; the devil, by contrast, or stray bits of our own unconscious make us less free, less whole, and they leave a nasty taste in the soul, however exciting the experience they produce at first. There need be no serious danger of confusing demonic or psychotic manifestations with the working of the Holy Spirit.

On the other hand, we must be well aware that the working of the Holy Spirit may not always conform to our ideas of propriety. If he really gets down to spring-cleaning the depths of our soul, some pretty unsavoury specimens are likely to be produced! The Spirit works on our nature, as it actually is, and that includes any hang-ups, blockages, obsessions, and so on, that we happen to have—all the raw material of mental break-down. We must never expect any manifestation of 'neat Holy Spirit'; there will always be an element of our own human spirit in any genuine manifestation of the Holy Spirit. That is what it is all about! It is us, as we are, that God is after. If it was only mediums he wanted, why bother with the whole sordid business of the Incarnation? In a disturbed personality the working of grace may at times look, and even *be*, hysterical or psychotic. What we should look for is not a spiritual perform-ance without hitch or blemish, but that whatever happens, sane or insane, is held within the love and healing power of the Spirit. In extreme cases, a breakdown may be the necessary preliminary to our spiritual breakthrough (cf. the writings of R. D. Laing and of Mary Barnes).[87] At all times, it is not the isolated phenomena we should judge, but their over-all direc-tion: are things moving simply towards ever deeper self-deception, masquerading as religion? Or is the pattern, finally, towards healing and wholeness, and the freedom of the sons of God? In other words, has Christ got his hand on it? If it is in *his* hands, who are we to get anxious?

As happened at Pentecost, someone speaking in tongues may turn out to be talking in some known language; even where this is not the case, there is generally some discernible linguistic pattern—one can distinguish between someone speaking in tongues, and someone simply making noises. Not that we should be unduly concerned about this—I do not see that there would be anything wrong in just making noises for God, if we felt like it! The only proviso, in either case, is that we must know how to *stop*, otherwise it can become mere self-indulgence, instead of being real prayer or praise.

A question that is often asked about tongues is, is it for everybody? Pentecostals are sometimes accused, not too unjustly, of trying to force tongues on everybody, and this no man has the right to do. St Paul's teaching is quite unambiguous, that we should not expect every christian to speak in tongues (I Corinthians 12:28). On the other hand, I do not believe that the Lord will refuse the gift to someone sincerely seeking it, in the full context of christian conversion, and with a genuine desire to serve the Lord.

But this does not yet quite answer the question. I think that, just as the fullness which is in Christ Jesus, given once and for all, is nevertheless unfolded, under the leading of the Holy Spirit, down the ages, and it is part of the prophetic awareness of the believer to discern where we have got to, so the individual must ask himself where he has got to, in the unfolding of the totality of grace given him at his baptism.

One part of that totality, one which we have seen reason to regard as pretty central, is precisely this prophetic awareness; it is so central that some spiritual writers have gone so far as to say that without it, in one form or another, you have not even begun. Sooner or later, there must come to most christians the challenge of the Spirit to enter into this inheritance. And when it comes, it may well be that the gift of tongues is the appointed doorway through which they must pass. The prophetic awareness, at least, is not an optional extra, even for those not called actually to pronounce the direct word of the Lord to other people. And tongues is still, as it was in the beginning, a normal, proper first step of prophecy.

And even those already well established under the yoke of faith and love, those well into contemplation, will find the gift of tongues a joy and a blessing, as well as providing them with another weapon of grace for their spiritual combat against 'principalities and powers and the world-rulers of this darkness' (Ephesians 6:12).

So how does one set about getting the gift of tongues? Well, you ask for it. Just place yourself in prayer, and, as simply as you can, pray to the Lord, who never refuses his Holy Spirit to us when we ask (Luke 11:13). Ask for tongues, and then, in faith, just *start*. You do the speaking, the Lord chooses the

words. You may find it helpful to get somebody else, or a
group, to pray with you, and lay hands on you, but this is not
essential. And if nothing happens at first, do not worry. It may
come to you in prayer a few hours later, or a few days; it may
take years. Don't worry, and don't turn back; you have made
your petition, now stick to it. Do not wonder whether you are
going to get it or not, or whether you have been wrong in
asking. 'Therefore I say to you, everything that you ask for in
prayer, believe that you have received it, and it will be yours'
(Mark 11:24). Continue to pray for it, and to yearn for it (the
Lord may hold it back for a time, to increase your desire), until
it is yours. The Lord himself will prompt you when the time is
ripe, both for the asking and for the receiving. Trust him, and
trust, relatively, the stirrings that you may feel in your heart.

Having once received the gift, we should persevere in it.
This can be hard, especially if one's first experience of tongues
has been sudden and exhilarating. Speaking in tongues is
generally a surprisingly matter-of-fact business. After a few
days, or a few weeks, it will almost certainly pall, it may even
become repugnant. It is, after all, a slap in the face for the old
Adam, and he will kick back with all the resources of the un-
converted subconscious. It is also a direct challenge to the
devil, and will not go unanswered. For this very reason, if for
no other, it is a good thing to persevere; and such perseverance
is rewarded, the joy does return, deeper and purified.

In speaking with other tongues, we surrender one little limb
to God's control. Ideally, this should help us more and more to
make ourselves over to him, gradually dispossessing ourselves
of ourselves, until finally he is our all in all, the centre of our
motivation, the source and goal of all that we are and do.

The end of this process is that we become filled with peace
and joy, that peace which passes all understanding, which
keeps our hearts and our minds in Christ Jesus (Philippians
4:7), that joy which no man can take away (John 16:22).

But this peace, this joy, is an acquired taste. The transition
from our old habits of anxiety, of not facing up to more than
half the truth of any situation, of relegating much of our lives
to a kind of resigned fatalism ('I'm only human', 'we all have
our faults'), the transition from this to the wholeness and per-

fection which are offered to us in Christ, may be intensely traumatic; we may feel that we are being torn in two (in fact, we probably are—cf. Hebrews 4:12; and the Lord warned us that he came, not to bring peace, but a sword (Matthew 10:34). God's peace is founded on absolute truth; it is a rock, on which such peace as the world offers is bound to founder).

After all, let's face it, we do not always really want peace, or even joy. 'A prison gets to be a friend,' as the American poetess, Emily Dickinson, observed. One of the Fathers talks of being 'drunk with thinking'[88], and this is surely a highly addictive style of intoxication. Our thoughts save us from ourselves, from our situation, from God.

So here is a dilemma. On the one hand, it is I who want to break through to the peace of Christ, in which to take his yoke upon me and learn of his gentleness and humility (Matthew 11:28f); but, on the other hand, it is also I who wish to stay 'drunk with thinking'. To pit one thought or desire against another will probably only give me a headache. So what is the answer?

'Duck!' says the author of the *Cloud of Unknowing*.[89] The way to get through the fog of thoughts is to sink down to a deeper level than thought or desire. The Greek Fathers recommend that we should turn to prayer of the heart, reciting the prayer of Jesus ('Lord Jesus Christ, Son of God, have mercy on me'), without thoughts. But tongues is even more precisely the tool for the job. It is a kind of prayer of the subconscious, that we can quite deliberately use against our own recalcitrant minds and wills, thus defeating ourselves, in a way, for God. It reaches beyond ourselves and our dilemma; in it the finger of God can reach down, through our thoughts and our conflicting desires, to that deeper level, where both thoughts and desires can be modulated and transformed, so building us up on the Rock which is Christ.

Many people can bear witness that, at a time of strain, praying in tongues can bring a great relief. Even if, at first, it seems only to make us more tense, if we go through with it, the outcome is triumph and glory. It is almost inevitable that, sometimes, we shall find ourselves, as it were, wrestling with God, his ways are so unlike our ways; but with whatever measure of freedom and faith we have, let us be quite determined that we shall take God's side against ourselves. In helping him to defeat us, paradoxically, we find peace and enhancement; if we hold out against him, we are sowing a storm and shall sooner or later have a whirlwind to reap.

In fact, praying in tongues is a weapon of war against the devil, and against our passions, precisely because it is a prayer of praise, a prayer of peace. God's peace is already established; in praise we assert it against all that is not peace. 'You have established praise . . . to destroy the enemy and the avenger' (Psalm 8:3 LXX). St Anthony tells how he once 'praised down' a demonic attack.[90] The battle is won in Christ; and it is our faith that makes real his victory in each particular situation. Praying in tongues is one act of faith that can very powerfully claim this victory and establish it effectively, whatever our need may be at the time.

And, of course, praise does not stop there. When we speak in tongues, we 'speak mysteries to God' (I Corinthians 14:2). Our words fail us; in tongues, our souls reach out to glorify God beyond anything we can ourselves comprehend. The English mystic, Walter Hilton, describes how the soul, when the fervour of its charity is sufficiently intense, becomes conscious of angel-song:[91] with the help of tongues, even we, who fall so far short of that intensity of love, can approximate to something of the same kind.

And the use of tongues is not confined to talking. It is possible to sing in tongues. Sometimes people receive the gift of 'singing in the Spirit' even before they can talk in tongues; this can happen to people who, naturally, cannot sing a note. It is a wonderful thing when a whole group starts singing in tongues. It can be a magnificent expression of praise and love, as well as a deep experience of fellowship with each other in the Lord. It can also bring a deep peace to a group and, if need be, can resolve a tense situation, or a spiritual impasse.

Speaking, and even more singing in tongues can be, in a curious way, a very authoritative kind of communication. It is as if words of power are being addressed to the very root of a problem, by-passing the normal mental intermediaries. Even without the gift of interpretation being used, there can be a very clear and imposing 'message' delivered this way, bearing immediate fruit in the group or the individual for whom it is intended.

Of course, tact must be used too. In a group which is familiar with the use of tongues, one can be much freer than in another group. The sheer human embarrassment caused by tongues could sometimes be sufficient to obviate any gain that would otherwise have resulted. The Lord may, on occasion, insist on tongues, regardless; but normally it is up to us to decide, prudently and charitably, whether and how to use tongues in a group.

Sometimes people insist rather vehemently on St Paul's rubrics in I Corinthians 14, even in informal groups, and will not allow much tongue-speaking, and never without inter-pretation, and never more than one person at a time. This is unfortunate, I think, and arises from a rather insidious con-fusion between liturgy and informal group prayer. St Paul's directives are intended to restore order in public worship in a congregation that had become divided and disorderly, and they do not apply equally, just like that, in the informal context of a small group at prayer. This is not, of course, an invitation to anarchy in prayer! But a group can, for instance, all be praising God at once, in tongues, even at the top of their voices, without it being a sign of disorder. A group must be conscious of its guests, of strangers in the midst, but, on the whole, I do not see why it should not enjoy all the freedom of private prayer. In fact, I think some groups get stuck at a very super-ficial level precisely because they formalise their prayer one way or another, and end up with nothing but fifth-rate liturgy. (This can happen in all kinds of ways: hymn sheets, rule of silence, rule of noise, organised meditations, almost anything, if you make a 'thing' of it.)

Prayer is the normal and principal purpose of the gift of tongues. But, on occasion, it is used also as a gift for preaching, and this is the use with which the scholastic theologians of the Middle Ages were familiar, and it is fairly widely attested among missionaries, ancient and modern, though it is often unclear whether the miracle is to be situated strictly in the speaking or in the hearing. St Vincent Ferrer, for instance,[92] and St. Francis

Xavier[93] both preached in languages they did not know, and the same thing is reported now from the mission field in our own century, though chiefly among Protestants, as far as I know.[94]

Those who receive the gift and persevere in it will discover for themselves its riches. It may not be the highest of gifts; and if it is not balanced with prayer of the understanding (I Corinthians 14:15), it can become simply self-indulgence. But even so, it made St Paul exclaim: 'I thank God that I speak in tongues more than you all!' (I Corinthians 14:18).

CHAPTER NINE

CONTEMPLATION AND MISSION

THE GIFT OF TONGUES should lead into the more public gifts of interpretation and, especially, prophecy.

'You will be my witnesses both in Jerusalem and in all Judea and Samaria, and right to the end of the earth' (Acts 1:8). 'As the Father has sent me, I also send you. . . . Receive the Holy Spirit' (John 20:21f). In their different ways, each of the evangelists (even the unexpanded Mark) concludes with some kind of experience of the risen, exalted Lord (this is the significance of the awe which fell upon the women in Mark 16:5 and 8), coupled with a command to go and tell people, to bear witness, whether by word or by example.

The church is, in fact, both called and sent: called to sanctity and salvation, and sent to preach the gospel to the whole creation (Mark 16:15), healing the sick and driving out demons (Matthew 10:8).

And it is only where action and contemplation have become secularised (or sacralised, for that matter—it comes to much the same thing), that any contradiction appears. It is only because we try to apprehend and practise prayer or good works without seeing how they proceed from the mission of Jesus Christ, that the hoary problem of reconciling and balancing the two arises.

In baptism we die with Christ and rise with him, receiving the Spirit that we may live no longer for sin and self, but for God. Of itself, this obviously does not entail any formally apostolic mission; but it certainly includes some kind of obligation to bear witness. 'To each is given the manifestation of the Spirit for the common good. To one is given, through the Spirit, the word of wisdom, and to another the word of knowledge, according to the same Spirit, to another faith, by the

same Spirit, to another gifts of healing by the one Spirit, to
another the working of miracles, to another prophecy. . . . All
these are effected by one and the same Spirit, distributing to
each one individually as he wills. For just as the body is one and
has many limbs, so it is with Christ. For we were all baptised in
one Spirit into one body' (I Corinthians 12:7–13).

Tertullian has surely grasped correctly the implication of
this, when he exhorts the newly baptised as they emerge from
the font, to pray for a 'distribution of charisms'.[95]

We are baptised, not simply into a community of salvation,
but also into a missionary body bearing witness to the Lordship
of Jesus Christ. As we enter more fully into the reality of our
baptism, our own mission within the church can be expected to
become clearer and more effective.

Now, as I have suggested, what contemplation is essentially
about is precisely the 'manifestation of baptism', the conscious
and free appropriation of God's working in us. If this is so,
there can be no genuine contemplation which is closed to
mission. And if, following Karl Rahner, we attempt to see
contemplation in rather more prophetic terms, the implication
becomes even clearer. As in Isaiah's famous experience, the
vision of God's glory leads straight into the question, 'Whom
shall I send?'

The Pentecostals, as we should expect, link mission, especially
charismatic mission, with 'baptism in the Spirit', which, for
them, is a man's personal Pentecost, distinguished fairly sharply
from the grace of conversion and water-baptism.

Using, often, the very same texts that the Pentecostals use,
Catholic theology too has sometimes made the same kind of
distinction, seeing baptism as the conferring of saving grace,
and confirmation as a man's commissioning to bear witness in
the power of the Spirit.

Confirmation is a notoriously difficult subject! Anything one
says on it, at present, can only, at best, be highly provisional.
However, it seems pretty clear that the typical Latin theory of
confirmation, like the Pentecostal theory of 'baptism in the
Spirit', evolved very much out of a particular historical situation. It is completely different, anyway, from the eastern
christian theory.

The most thorough scriptural and patristic research (especially the work of Prof. G. W. H. Lampe and, more recently, Dr J. D. Dunn)[96] tends to draw the emphasis very much back to the unity of the one initiatory event of repentance and baptism. In the older practice, baptism and confirmation were not separated, and this is still normal in the eastern churches. The Vatican Council insisted in emphatic terms that their practice should be retained, and further decreed that the Latin rite of confirmation should be revised 'in order that the intimate connection of this sacrament with the whole of christian initiation may appear more clearly'.[97] It seems that adult converts are normally to receive both sacraments at once.

So we do not have to, and indeed should not seek to make too sharp a distinction between sanctification and mission. Rather, they are two aspects of the one life given to us by Christ in the Holy Spirit. The unfolding of this one life cannot be fitted to a blueprint; moral transformation, public witness, charismatic ministry, contemplative prayer, all these are involved, but in what degree and order they will grow cannot be determined in advance.

It is true, all the same, that there are two things we can distinguish. There are the specific ministries within the church, at least some of which begin at a definite point in time subsequent to baptism. And there is also the witnessing which consists simply in the kind of transformed life that the christians live (see especially John 13:35 and 17:23. It is interesting that John never once uses the word 'preach'). These two complement each other. We may even see in the fact that we do have *two* sacraments evidence that both are necessary and essential parts of the life in Christ.

It is greatly to the credit of the Pentecostals that they have systematically sought to revive the whole range of ministries in the church, and we can ill afford to spurn this lesson. However, the more Johannine emphasis on the perfecting of our own lives in love is just as important. As John Wesley said, 'the work of God does not prosper where perfect love is not preached'.[98]

'If I speak with the tongues of men and of angels, without having love, I am a noisy gong or a clanging cymbal. If I have prophecy and know all mysteries and all knowledge, and if I

have complete faith so as to move mountains, but without
having love, I am nothing. And if I give away all my posses-
sions and hand over my body to be burned, but without having
love, I gain nothing' (I Corinthians 13:1–3). St Paul is not
recommending love instead of tongues, prophecy, good works;
he bids us seek such things. Nor is he denying the reality of the
various phenomena of moral and social excellence, mystical
knowledge and miraculous powers. Only, in his view, the
phenomena, of themselves, have no christian significance at all.
Deeper than all the phenomena is love, and it is love that
validates all our moral and religious acts; it is love that makes
them christian.

And St Paul does not mean simply a human sentiment of
love. There is more to the man who gives away all his goods,
but without love, than simply wrong human motivation. Love,
for St Paul, the love which makes things christian, is the love
poured out in our hearts by the Holy Spirit.

And 'in this is love: not that we have loved God. but that he
loved us, and sent his Son as a propitiation for our sins' (I John
4:10). The love which makes our contemplation, our good
works, our miracles, christian, is not, in the first place, a fact
about us at all, it is a fact about God. Deeper even than the
phenomenon of human love, is the fact of God's love, the fact
of Jesus Christ.

And here we touch the very nub of the christian mystery.
Deeper than our ministries and works, deeper than our prayer
and contemplation, lies the reality of God's everlasting Will, the
eternal generation of his Son, in that inconceivable ecstasy of
love which is the Holy Spirit proceeding from them both; in
which already, from before all time, the Father also wills his
whole creation and all that is or will be in it. That we should
love and know is only a function of our being loved and being
known.

This means that we can base our lives on nothing in ourselves,
however sanctified. It is man's peculiar privilege to be nothing
in himself; it is only in so far as we transcend ourselves, that we
can make sense of ourselves. We may transcend ourselves into
the world, letting the world construct and interpret us. Or we
may let God mould us. And we cannot serve two masters: we

have to choose. And to opt for God is, in principle, to opt for living wholly on his terms, and that means living at a level deeper than ourselves, deeper than anything we can really comprehend.

This means, on the one hand, a total detachment from phenomena of all kinds. If we work, we must not depend on success, and we must be prepared to give up working. Similarly, if we pray, we must not look for success, and we must, in a sense, be prepared to give up praying. It has been said that one test of true prayer is one's readiness to be disturbed and called away from prayer. The Spirit is as unaccountable as the wind.

On the other hand, we must be prepared to take all phenomena in our stride. The principle of unity in our lives is quite simply God's will, transforming our will into his own. This is the answer to the problem, so vexed in all the manuals of spirituality, how to combine love of God with love of neighbour. The problem is illusory. The fundamental thing is not my love at all, but God's love. My love for God is a function of his own divine love; my love for other people is a function of *his* love for them. 'The love of me,' as the Lord said to St Catherine, 'and the love of your neighbour are one and the same thing, and to the extent that the soul loves me, it loves him too, because its love towards him emanates from me.'[99] In everything it is God who works in us 'both to will and to work' (Philippians 2:13). So, just as in prayer we must seek to pray the prayers that God gives us, so in action we must seek to do the good works 'that God has prepared for us to walk in' (Ephesians 2:10). This is the love that validates our prayer and our activities; it is not a matter of our motivation, but of the reality of Jesus Christ, who is the Will of the Father.

Just as the Father sent Christ, even so he sends us; and so we cannot opt out of the 'greater works than these' which he promised us that we should do (John 14:12). Healing the sick, and casting out demons, and even raising the dead, are part of the job given to the church (Matthew 10:8). 'In this house of yours' (as the rite for the consecration of a church says) 'we pray you, Lord, by the grace of the Holy Spirit, may the sick be cured, the infirm restored, the lame healed, lepers cleansed, and the blind given sight, and may demons be cast out.' It is not for us to decide that we are unworthy to do such things. What makes us think ourselves worthy to do the things that we *do* do, anyway?

When St Catherine said to the Lord on one occasion, 'I am not worthy,' he replied, 'No, but I am worthy.' [100]

In 850 a local church council at Pavia in northern Italy specially bid the clergy preach the sacrament of the sick 'by which sins are forgiven, and so bodily health is restored'.[101] The Council of Trent—surprisingly, in view of the opinions expressed during the previous debate—actually passed a canon anathematising anyone who should claim that the anointing of the sick 'does not relieve the sick, but has now lapsed—as if the gift of healings (*gratia curationum*) were exclusively a thing of the past'.[102] At last, since the Second Vatican Council, there are signs that the church is really beginning to pay serious attention once more to her healing ministry, both sacramental and charismatic.

The ministry of exorcism, unfortunately, still seems sadly neglected in the catholic church, in spite of an exemplary lead given by the Church of England. At a time when so many are dabbling in spiritualism and magic and diverse kinds of occultism, it is particularly lamentable that the church pays so little attention to her battle against demonic powers. This too is part of our job, whether it appeals to our Weltanschauung or not.

It would be tedious to relate in detail the various ministries in the church that have largely gone into abeyance, or at least underground. What is vital is that we grasp the principle of all ministries, official or unofficial, spectacular or unspectacular. The vital root of all christian action, as of all christian prayer, is the will of God. And this is something that cannot be judged by the standards of the world. In so far as we act as christians, we act, humanly speaking, unjustifiably. This is, of course, typical of prophetic action, and, as we saw, all christians are called, at least in this sense, to be prophets. We must be prepared to do things that we cannot explain, to say things that we cannot really back up. We must be ready to act, to speak, to pray, on the authority of God himself.

One absolutely fundamental tenet of christianity, and one from which—in spite of St Ignatius' best endeavours—we keep trying to run away, is that God can get through to us, direct.

God's revelation is not confined to the general teaching of the church, the moral and theological principles given publicly for everyone; he also shows himself to each one of us in particular, in so far as we are willing to look. Increasingly, the christian should be one who is led by the Spirit; whose motivation, therefore, becomes more and more inscrutable, even to himself, whose activity is likely to look more and more wayward (compare John 3:8, again!). It is not enough for him simply to look around the world and see what needs to be done; he must seek to discover what God is giving him to do. He must learn to refrain from working, so that God can show him his proper work. And he must not judge by outward criteria of success or failure (the crucifixion did not exactly look like success). He must abandon himself more and more to God's unaccountable ways, with little to assure him that he is on the right track, except that, somehow, it *is* right.

And, of course, this does not mean illuminism. 'The wisdom that is from above is peaceful, gentle, open to reason' (James 3:17). Divine guidance draws together into harmony all our various levels of knowledge and intuition, and leads to a quiet confidence, far removed from the stubbornness and contentiousness of the man who is merely opinionated.

In fact, one who is truly moved and sent by God is about as unlike as possible to the man who 'has a mission in life', in the popular sense.

> 'See, my servant whom I have chosen,
> my beloved in whom my soul delights,
> I will lay my Spirit upon him
> and he will proclaim justice to the nations.
> He will not wrangle or shout,
> nor will people hear his voice in the streets.
> He will not break a bruised reed
> or quench a smouldering wick,
> until he has brought justice to victory.
> And the nations will hope in his name.'

St Matthew uses this text from Isaiah (Isaiah 42:1–4; Matthew 12:15–21) to explain why Jesus kept withdrawing and refusing to let himself be made into a public figure, a motif that occurs in all the gospels, but which seems to have been especially meaningful to Matthew.

This picture of the true servant of the Lord contrasts forcibly with those splendid Jewish revivalists, the Pharisees, who 'crossed land and sea to make a single convert' (Matthew 23:15). St Matthew, with his Essene background, was especially anti-Pharisee, and we must take a pinch of salt from our other evidence, with his abuse. St Paul, himself once a Pharisee, shows us their enormous strength and zeal for the Lord (Philippians 3:3ff). If they were 'hypocrites', making a great show of their religion, their aim—like that of their modern counterparts—was to testify for God. They behaved as they did because their religion was important to them; only their zeal was of no use, because it was 'without knowledge. For not knowing God's justice and seeking to establish a justice of their own, they did not subject themselves to God's justice' (Romans 10:2f).

The saints too have always been ready to preach 'in season, out of season' (II Timothy 4:2), but first they seek to be constantly aware that they are themselves the prodigal come home, in whose honour the whole court of heaven is holding a party. God's justice is not that of the stern moralist (the older brother in the parable), it does not 'preach at' people; it is that of the father who runs out in haste to welcome back sinners, that of the good shepherd who leaves the ninety-nine sheep to go out and look for the one that has got lost.

There is a kind of reticence about the saints, like the reticence of the Lord himself, and it is this that makes them able truly to do God's work and to speak his word, without making people feel threatened or 'got at' by them, without crushing the bruised reed or extinguishing the smouldering wick.

They rejoice to be disciplined as an army (II Timothy 2:4), yet free as the wind (John 3:8) and carefree as birds (Matthew 6:26), and so their light shines out before men and *cannot* be hidden (Matthew 5:14). The truly spiritual man is characterised by a calm and profound realism and detachment. Because he has decided to let God be God, he can forgo cares and ambitions; he can surrender the luxury of ideology, with all its attendant righteous indignation. He does not have to constrain the world to prove his point.

In this state, a Biafran child is simply a Biafran child, not the proof of a political theory; a Bengali refugee is simply a Bengali refugee, and as such can be loved with a pure love, barbed by no selfish intent. The spiritual man, because he is not trying to make a point, never has to make anyone feel 'got at' by his charity. ('What good is charity where there is arrogance?' as abba Elias asks).[103] He has, in a sense, dispensed with theories. He acts with sublime authority—as it was said of St Dominic that, having once made up his mind about something, he hardly ever changed it.[104] But the result is not tyranny or arrogance, but an amazing purity and accuracy of love. And this is because human motivation is swallowed up in divine motivation. And God's love sets us truly free. Our love finds its fulfilment in being transformed into God's love, and only then will our works be truly fruitful.

CHAPTER TEN

THE EVIDENCE OF THE SPIRIT

W E HAVE NOW CONSIDERED all the basic elements in the Pentecostal doctrine of 'baptism in the Spirit', allowing them to highlight certain features of our own spiritual tradition in the catholic church of east and west, and to remind us of things we had been in danger of forgetting.

It is now time for us to take stock and, provisionally, attempt to view the matter once more as a whole. The crucial question for us is: can we accept the doctrine of 'baptism in the Spirit'? And if not, how are we to cope, theologically and pastorally, with the experience or experiences that go under that name?

Let us just recall what the doctrine is. After conversion (which we attest, the Pentecostals say, by submitting to water-baptism), there is something *more* for us, namely baptism in the Spirit, in which we receive the fullness of the Spirit. According to the strict, original Pentecostal doctrine, this reception of the Spirit is attested by our speaking in tongues. (They like to say that at our conversion we bear witness to God by submitting to water-baptism; in 'baptism in the Spirit' God bears witness to us, by making us speak in tongues.)[105] The neo-Pentecostals, however, have tended on the whole not to demand tongues, or, indeed, any immediate manifestation.

The Catholic Pentecostals, I think it is fair to add, do not accept the Pentecostal reduction of the sacrament of baptism to mere 'water-baptism',[106] though, so far as I know, they do not seem particularly concerned that this might have repercussions on the doctrine of Spirit-baptism.

The doctrine, as doctrine, rests on certain texts from the Book of Acts, which are alleged to show (i) that there is a second experience after conversion (salvation), (ii) that this second experience consists of the full reception of the Spirit, and (iii) that this is the fulfilment of the prophecy of John the Baptist, and is to be viewed therefore as the promised baptism in the Holy Spirit. Classic Pentecostals add (iv) that there is an initial evidence of the reception of the Spirit, and this initial evidence is speaking in tongues.

In chapter five I gave reasons for not accepting the Pentecostal exegesis of the relevant passages, as well as alleging other texts that seem to belie their claims. The full scriptural pattern, I suggested, shows rather that the Holy Spirit is received precisely in conversion, in the gift of *metanoia*, the new life in Christ, and that this is experienced and evidenced sacramentally in baptism, in which we are born again 'of water and the Holy Spirit' (John 3:5). In baptism we enter mystically into the whole reality of Christ's death and resurrection and his exaltation to the right hand of glory to receive the Holy Spirit.

The case has most recently been argued, and argued very cogently, by Prof. F. D. Bruner, the second part of whose book is a systematic study of the 'Pentecostal' texts. He concludes, as I had already, independently, concluded, that these very texts teach precisely the unity of the gift of the Spirit; the situation in Acts 8 is reported to emphasise the abnormality of a baptism which does not lead to a manifest reception of the Spirit (Luke, by and large, being uninterested in any secret working of the Spirit; we should avoid interpolating Pauline considerations into Luke's story). St Paul's question to the Ephesian disciples in Acts 19 is very illuminating: 'Did you receive the Spirit *when you believed*?' (the Authorised Version is misleading here, and has misled many Pentecostals; there is no justification whatsoever in the Greek text for the rendering 'since ye believed'). In response to their confession of ignorance, he asks straight away: 'into what then *were you baptised*?' The implication could hardly be clearer. As Bruner concludes, 'baptism is the sure visible evidence taught in Acts of the reception of the forgiveness of sins with the co-ordinate gift of the Holy Spirit'. 'Baptism is the Spirit's own sufficient evidence.'[107]

This does not mean that the New Testament has no interest in other manifestations of the Spirit. Obviously it has! All that is being claimed is that baptism is the appointed locus, the appointed 'visibility', of reception of the Spirit. We should neither exaggerate this claim, as sacramentalists have tended to do, nor reduce it, as evangelicals and especially Pentecostals have tended to do. There is a great diversity of ways in which the Spirit works in us; the one thing that is common to all, and is the bond of our unity, is baptism. This is why baptism, rather than tongues, or exultation, or any other operation of the Spirit, features in St Paul's great plea for unity in the letter to the Ephesians: 'try to keep the unity of the Spirit in the bond of peace, one body and one Spirit, just as you were called to a single hope; one Lord, one faith, one baptism, one God and Father of all' (Ephesians 4:3–6). This is why in all the ancient creeds, in the section devoted to the Holy Spirit, we profess belief in the one church and the one baptism for the remission of sins.

The New Testament does not, then, really substantiate the claim that there is something *more*, something subsequent to conversion and baptism, in which we receive the fullness of the Spirit in some special, absolute way. There can certainly be a new filling with the Spirit subsequent to one's first reception of the Spirit, as Acts 4:31 bears witness; but there is no single, second event. It is in christian baptism that the Baptist's prophecy finds its fulfilment.

Scripture, then, does not teach a Pentecostal 'second blessing'. Furthermore, the theological tradition of the church, nourished by scripture and the experience of christians down the ages, strongly resists any suggestion that christian baptism is a mere 'water-baptism', like that of John, foreshadowing a second, more powerful, 'Spirit-baptism'. The New Testament texts about baptising in the Spirit, in so far as they have become part of the general theological language of the church at all, have found their place in a sacramental context. It is in the church's baptism that Jesus baptises with the Holy Spirit. (For what it is worth, it is interesting that St Thomas uses the term *baptisma flaminis, scilicet Spiritus Sancti*, 'baptism of the Holy Spirit', to refer to 'baptism of desire', the inner baptism vouchsafed to one who sincerely wants to be born again, but, for whatever reason, is unable to be baptised outwardly.[108] St Catherine of Siena uses the term 'baptism of fire' in the same sense.[109])

There are strong scriptural and theological reasons, then, for not believing in a 'baptism in the Holy Spirit', such as is alleged by the Pentecostals.

But this cannot be the end of the story; the reality of their experience forces us to look further. And we should not be too dismayed to find that the exegetical and theological ground has been cut from under our feet.

For a long time catholics used the Vulgate translation of Luke 1:28 (*gratia plena*, 'full of grace') as the basis for a whole understanding of the rôle of Mary in mediating all grace to us. Now that we cannot use that particular text any longer, we find that our understanding of Mary's mediation, far from being shattered, is considerably enriched (see, for instance, the relevant section of the Vatican Council's *Constitution on the Church*).

Similarly with the papacy, now that its claim on Matthew 16:18f is being weakened.

And, as a matter of historical fact, in both cases the doctrine preceded the exegesis; we read the bible, inevitably, in the light of our experience of what it means to be a christian.

The Pentecostals objectified and interpreted their experience in the light of John the Baptist's prophecy and certain texts from Acts. We cannot accept their interpretation, and we may not be able to accept their objectification (what they refer to under one name may turn out to be a multiplicity of different realities); but that does not entitle us simply to reject their experience.

The Spirit, the gift of the new life in Christ, comes to us at baptism. There is nothing *more* than this, all is contained within the one reality of *metanoia*. If we are in Christ at all, there is a 'new creation', and everything is ours. We should not aim at 'christianity plus'; that is the royal road to heresy, as St Paul already has to warn some of his churches (the Colossians, for instance). As against the heretics, as Tertullian rather quaintly puts it, we are God's 'little fish, who remain in the water in which we are born', resisting the allurements of those who would pull us out from the font.[110]

Christianity plus is, as Bruner insists, no longer christianity.[111] But mystical movements, like Pentecostalism, arise precisely in protest against christianity *minus*. In so far as they seek to bring people to an authentic experience of the 'new creation' in Christ, and so to get beyond a tepid and worldly christianity, that has lost its purpose, they are surely sound and even necessary to the church.

We are bidden to 'be perfect as your heavenly Father is perfect'. In baptism we receive the sacrament of perfection— the 'perfect' being, in fact, one ancient designation for those who had been baptised, to distinguish them from the catechumens awaiting baptism. In baptism we receive the Holy Spirit, the 'perfecter'.[112] But this perfection clearly does not become fully operative all at once. The christian life is our attempt to live into the perfection received sacramentally, under the continual guidance and inspiration of the same Spirit that we received at the outset.

There is one ancient and quite respectable tradition, according to which, as we try to live faithfully following the practices of the church and such special graces as we may receive, we enter gradually ever more deeply into the mysteries of Christ, without any dramatic or critical turning points on the way.

But for many people this is, unfortunately, not enough; their way needs to be more clearly articulated. Accordingly, in God's providence, there have arisen from time to time schools of spirituality, which spell out various stages of spiritual growth, and various experiences that people will pass through. Their teaching may be very simple, or very complicated. Arintero mentions one school which specifies fifteen stages, and even so does not reach to the heights of supernatural prayer.[113] St Teresa of Ávila has a sevenfold scheme.[114] At the other extreme, most evangelicals and some eastern christians seem to be concerned only with one definite and decisive experience. This seems to be true of the Catholic Pentecostals too. Other Pentecostals point to two critical experiences, as did the Holiness movements and the early Methodists. St John of the Cross and, in fact, the commonest teaching of eastern and western christians, see the christian life in three stages too, though, unlike the Pentecostals, they are less concerned with precise, datable experiences, and talk rather of stages, each of which can be clearly distinguished by its characteristic range of experiences and 'evidences'; the transition from one stage to another may be sudden and dramatic, or long and obscure (which is what the 'dark nights' in St John of the Cross are all about).

Now it is quite in order to see these various stages, these various experiences, as distinct gifts and graces of the Holy Spirit. We can expect and pray to receive and to be filled with the Spirit any number of times; indeed, according to St Luke, this is the chief object of prayer (Luke 11:13). And one effect of receiving the Spirit is precisely that we should *know* the gift that has been given to us (I Corinthians 2:12), and this surely has relevance to the unfolding in our experience and consciousness of the grace given sacramentally in baptism.

It is also quite proper that the stages and experiences spelled out in the various schools of spirituality should be clearly identifiable by definite 'signs'[115] or 'evidences',[116] whether the 'baptism of tears' beloved of Symeon, or the 'ligature' associated with the prayer of quiet in western mysticism. And it is desirable that these signs and evidences should be as unambiguous as possible; the Pentecostal insistence on the 'physical sign of tongues' is far more satisfactory than Wesley's 'most infallible of proofs, inward feeling',[117] and far less exposed to the danger of illuminism.

The purpose of all these systems is to objectify certain experiences, by providing a framework of conceptual support and interpretation; this can help to indicate the significance of these experiences for the christian life, together with appropriate warnings and encouragements. But we must not forget that this objectification is only relative, like the grid upon the map. Experiences are interpreted in the context of a particular system of spirituality, in its own language, with its own concepts; outside, they might mean something quite different, or nothing at all. A spiritual director on Mount Athos need know no more of the 'ligature' than a Carmelite director need know of the 'baptism of tears' and 'prayer of the heart'; and neither is necessarily one whit the poorer for it.

What we must avoid—as indeed Wesley pointed out[118]—is turning any spiritual experience into a 'shibboleth'. All the great spiritual writers have warned us that there is a great danger in any spiritual experience, any spiritual advance that

befalls us, that we shall then turn to judge everybody else who
has not had the same experience. We have had a great conversion experience, so we require the same of everybody else
before we will call them christian. We have had a great experience of the Holy Spirit, so we want everyone else to have
the same experience before they can qualify as 'Spirit-filled'.

This is really the most serious objection of all to the Pentecostal doctrine of 'baptism in the Holy Spirit'. By claiming that
their particular kind of experience *is* (in some absolute sense)
reception of the fullness of the Spirit, they inevitably make a
shibboleth out of it, and this shows in their very invidious
use of the term 'Spirit-filled'. For this there is no scriptural,
theological or pastoral justification.

Unfortunately, there is some confusion within Pentecostalism
itself here. The first Pentecostals, still close to their roots in the
Holiness Movement, supposed that complete sinlessness was a
pre-condition of 'baptism in the Holy Spirit.'[119] If we are going
to talk at all about 'fullness of the Spirit', in some special sense,
surely this would be it: we might say that we receive the Spirit
sacramentally at baptism, and then the fullness of the Spirit
when we reach actual perfection.

But then the Pentecostals added their own distinctive doctrine of tongues as the 'initial evidence' of reception of the Holy
Spirit. Now I am sure that there is very good reason indeed for
insisting on some kind of evidence, and this is fully borne out
by almost all traditions of spirituality in the church; on that, I
am at one with the classic Pentecostals against most of the
neo-Pentecostals. The only trouble is that tongues cannot
possibly serve as evidence of perfection, of entire sinlessness. As
we saw earlier, no charismatic gift as such is evidence of any
degree of sanctification at all, let alone complete sanctification.

There is no justification for supposing that anyone who
receives the gift of tongues has received any special 'fullness of
the Spirit'. The gift of tongues is certainly an evidence of the
Spirit, and, as I have suggested, can have a very important rôle
in our spiritual development; but it is quite compatible with
considerable spiritual immaturity. As St Thomas says, so bluntly
as to be almost untranslatable, 'although prophecy (and the
same would apply to tongues) is a gift of the Holy Spirit, never-

theless it is not with the gift of prophecy that the Holy Spirit is given, but the gift of charity'.[120] For all their tongue-speaking, St Paul could not address the Corinthians as 'spiritual' people at all (I Corinthians 3:1), and much harm can be done by parading our spiritual immaturity as 'the fullness of the Spirit'. It does no good either to us or to those whom we propose to help or inspire.

There are many experiences of the Spirit, and since scripture does not support the contention that there is one, special, privileged experience, we should not seek to oversimplify or over-objectify the situation. What neo-Pentecostals, at any rate, generally mean by 'baptism in the Spirit', far from being the gift of entire sanctification or perfection, is a kind of initiatory experience of the Holy Spirit, a beginning of contemplation. Dr Josephine Massingberd Ford, in fact, who is a Catholic Pentecostal, has said that it is a 'touch of infused contemplation'.[121] It has, rather aptly, been called in the Greek tradition 'the discovery of the Spirit'. It may be a person's first real experience of God and of faith.

This initial experience of the Holy Spirit is important. It is not enough that we should know 'by hearsay' that we have been baptised. For those who feel that they have never really got off the ground yet, it may be helpful to learn that there can be a definite experience of 'discovery of the Spirit' or 'manifestation of baptism'. And this initial experience may well involve reception of the gift of tongues (for tongues as an evidence of conversion and faith, see Acts 11:17). At least, it is quite proper that we should stress praise and prophecy, with or without tongues, as an important and characteristic evidence of the Spirit.

This is one definite and important kind of experience of the Spirit. We should be prepared to lead people to it, if this is their way, and we should be aware of the consequences of it in a person's life.

But there are plenty of other experiences of the Spirit, and we should never judge anyone devoid of the Spirit because he has not come our way; nor should we write him off as hopelessly reprobate because he declines to come our way. Who are we to judge the servants of the Lord (cf. Romans 14:4)?

Nor should we forget those who are no longer beginners in the ways of the Lord. One of the hazards of Pentecostalism is that, due to the way it presents itself, and especially its doctrine of 'baptism in the Spirit', it appears to have nothing to say to those who already have some experience of the Spirit. It has so over-objectified one particular kind of experience of the Spirit, that it has almost no account to give of others. This means that when Pentecostals meet others who manifestly do know something of the Holy Spirit, they either have to claim them as being already 'baptised in the Spirit', which does not much help a person who is, perhaps, genuinely seeking some further inspiration and help from them. Or they deny that he is 'baptised in the Spirit', and implicitly deny the value of what he has already experienced. This does not help him either.

In fact, however advanced we may be in the Lord's service, however mature spiritually, there is always more for us, and we should pray for it; not undervaluing what we have already, but pressing on to perfection. In St Bernard's view, 'there is no proof of the presence of the Spirit which is more certain than a desire for ever greater grace'.[122] We need always to pray to receive the Holy Spirit. And at times there may be a quite specific prayer we should pray.

We may quite profitably pray for the gift of tongues, not, this time, as a sign of spiritual breakthrough, as a 'discovery of the Spirit', but as a gift for prayer and service.

Or we may need to pray for the Spirit in order to overcome some particular obstacle in ourselves that has been brought to light by the working of grace in us; it may be some habit of mistrust, or fear, or ill-will, that the Lord wants to tackle in us. We can and should pray for a definite working of grace here.

We may simply feel moved to pray for perfection, and to that end we should pray for a renewed, indeed a continually renewed, outpouring of the Holy Spirit.

But, whatever our prayer, we should pray precisely. For a beginner, prayer for a 'baptism in the Holy Spirit' will clearly mean prayer for the 'discovery of the Spirit', and, simply from this point of view, the terminology may do no harm. But thereafter it can be nothing but an escape from the real prayer that is needed. People can pray for a 'baptism in the Spirit' and have thousands of people lay hands on them, and nothing will ever happen, because their prayer means nothing. They are not really asking for anything. They have already had their 'honeymoon' with the Lord, and are not going to get another. They do not, perhaps, want tongues. And instead of facing up to the real blockage in their souls, that the Lord wants to remove, instead of identifying the particular door in their hearts at which the Lord is knocking, they take refuge in grandiose talk of 'baptism in the Spirit', successfully evading the real issue to which the Lord is trying to bring them. They have the appearance of prayer, but I am afraid it means nothing. Bad doctrine has led them astray.

So we cannot, for scriptural, theological and pastoral reasons, accept the Pentecostal doctrine of 'baptism in the Spirit', and we should avoid the term. Nor should we simply substitute some other term; we must recognise that there is a diversity of experiences of the Spirit, and we should be more precise and subtle in our teaching.

On the other hand, we must accept squarely the challenge as to what we know of the Spirit's working in us. We should pray to receive the Spirit, not simply as a pious duty, but with the eager expectation that things will happen. And we should not be afraid to lead people to an initial experience, if this is appropriate, and we should not forget the possibility of tongues. We should be insistent on praise and thanksgiving.

But we should never make anyone feel inferior because they have had no such experience, nor should we bring moral pressure to bear on people to seek an experience that they do not want, and will not be able to assimilate.

As John Wesley put it, we should be 'always drawing rather than driving'.[123]

In the last analysis, it is not the *experience* of God that we must preach, but his reality. Our hope, stored up for us in heaven, is no less than the man Jesus Christ himself, the Son of God, made man for our salvation.

CHAPTER ELEVEN

ICONS AND IDOLS

WE CANNOT, it appears, simply accept Pentecostalism at its face value. But we can learn from it a way of spirituality, and a mass of 'case-law' in spiritual matters; their stories are, in fact, as exciting and helpful as those of the Russian *startsi* or the Desert Fathers or the early mendicants. We must, I think, see Pentecostalism as one of the many mystical movements of our age, one which has sprung up within christianity, and which offers a genuine possibility of renewal in the Spirit of Jesus Christ.

But we must know how to cope with mysticism, and this is where the sound theology is so important. Even when it arises within the church, mysticism is not intrinsically christian; but it can be made christian.

And we must also be well aware that the devil has his well-tried ways of containing and taking the sting out of all moves towards renewal and a fuller embodiment of the gospel. Every divine initiative towards us is dogged by the devil's counter-attack, and we need to understand his tactic.

In fact, right from the start, christianity was seen in terms of a great conflict with spirits of evil. Exorcism was regarded as one of the chief evidences of the truth of the gospel.

Two things were especially regarded as works of the devil, and against them the church battled and testified with all her might: oracles, and idolatry. These were seen as the typical products of the devil. In a more modern guise, I think these are still his typical products, and our conflict is still in large measure against them. Oracles give a too ready answer, idols a too facile comfort. They make us feel religious, but without unsettling us; they allow us to remain quite at home in the world. They are, in fact, the religion of the 'Prince of this world'.

We saw in the last chapter the danger of over-objectifying certain spiritual experiences—and we might have added, certain doctrines too. We must now see that this danger is precisely the danger of idolatry. An idol is a god, or a manifestation of god, or an experience of god, or a doctrine of god, that one has 'made a thing of'.

It is important to understand how idols are made. Of course, there are the gross idols, like money, reputation, sex; everyone knows about them. But the worst idols are the ones which tend to escape observation, because they are made out of genuinely religious, even christian, material. It is these I want to draw attention to now.

Christianity is a religion of incarnation. The fullness towards which we aspire is found in its perfection in the human flesh of Jesus. Every move towards the realisation in us of that fullness in Christ involves an element of embodiment. The sacraments, religious practices, the scriptures, all these embody in different ways our union with Christ. To say that they are means is not intended to disparage them; they mediate the wholeness of the Christ who is larger than they. But, precisely because of this, no single one of them can ever be indispensable. St Thomas goes as far as any oriental in insisting that all these things are only *props*, leading to and flowing from the transcendent reality of the living grace of the Holy Spirit.[124] They are intended as icons. The devil tries to turn them into idols, so that we will become so satisfied with the means, that we forget the end. The icon embodies for us a reality far greater than itself; in so far as it is such an embodiment, we treasure and revere it. But we do not get hung up on it; Christ is larger than his media of communication, and so we too must be free with regard to them. If we do get hung up on them, they become idols, which claim to contain their own reality. They opt out of transcendence. And then they can serve the devil in either direction: if we keep them, he has us bound. If we reject them, we are easily duped into spiritualising our religion, so that it ceases to have any bodily reality at all, and then becomes irrelevant and ineffective in our actual lives. We implicitly deny that Christ has come in the flesh.

We can see the whole process clearly in the first christian

centuries. At first it was martyrdom: earnest lovers of our Lord yearned for this full bodily identification with him in his passion. But then it got short-circuited. People who were not spiritually ready for it volunteered themselves for martyrdom, and then had not the strength to see it through, giving great scandal to all. The church had to be very precise, insisting that martyrdom was not something *more* than being a christian, it was a very direct embodiment of being a christian, a mirror held up to the face of each believer. But nevertheless, it was not co-extensive with the idea of being a christian.

Then it was asceticism. As martyrdom became less likely, earnest souls undertook voluntary hardships out of their desire for simpler, closer union with Christ. Asceticism was their way of giving body to their devotion. It was not a way of being christian *plus*, it was their way of being a christian. But again, it got short-circuited. Asceticism became an end in itself, the icon became an idol. Much of our early monastic writing is concerned to put asceticism in its place.

Perhaps the most interesting case of all, for our purposes, is in fact monasticism, which Henri Brémond actually called 'a second Pentecost'.[125] In face of a church going cold and respectable, people like Anthony simply dropped out into the desert, in response to the simplicity and directness of the gospel challenge. Their move of utter faith was embodied in a total renunciation of worldly concern and security; and it was rewarded by a living awareness of the Holy Spirit, and a life open to the charismatic and the miraculous. 'What is better than having the Holy Spirit?' as abba Theodore remarked.[126] 'We believe that all things are possible to God: well then, believe it in your own life, that God can work miracles in you too' (abba Euprepius).[127] They did not think that they were being anything other than straightforward christians; in fact, they were inclined to talk as if they had only become christians at the time of their dropping-out, their 'renunciation' (a word with baptismal connotations). In a sense, this was true, for them: their renunciation gave body and reality to their baptismal faith.

But the devil wasn't going to leave it at that. Their move of gospel faith became institutionalised as a special way, as christianity *plus*. Where Cassian teaches that monastic renunciation leads into the freedom of the new law, the law of love, the Holy Spirit, Caesarius of Arles turns it hideously upside down, offering a theology of the laity in terms precisely of the old law![128] The church has still not recovered from this.

Exactly the same thing happened with contemplation. The early writers never dreamed that they were concerned with anything other than the living reality of the gospel of Jesus Christ. In evolving techniques and practices of spirituality, they were aiming to give body to the christian faith. But once again, somehow, mysticism came to be a highly esoteric matter, reserved, at least in practice, for a small élite. It proved quite in vain, as we have seen, to assert from within an already esoteric mystical theology, that it was not meant to be esoteric. It had already lost contact both with the rest of theology (sacramental, moral, scriptural, dogmatic) and with most believers.

In each case it is the same ploy: a move of the Spirit to lead men into the full experience of the redemption in Christ, in all its simplicity, gets trapped and turned into an idol. It becomes esoteric, and therefore does not reach nearly as many people as it might, and tends to corrupt those whom it does reach, with complacency and spiritual pride (if not downright schism). In seeking to be something *more* than mere christianity, it ends up with considerably less, while at the same time lulling its adepts into a false sense of security; it makes them feel that going through certain motions is a kind of spiritual guarantee. According to St Thomas, there is no such guarantee, even where the motions in question are certainly supernatural, as with the sacraments and with phenomena 'in spirit'.[129]

We must never allow the radical and agonising questing of the human heart for God, the questing of God himself for man, to be trivialised into the mere doing of certain things, saying of certain words, feeling of certain emotions. God wants to seduce us into the desert, there to speak tenderly to us (Hosea 2:14); the devil tries the whole time to turn God's very allurements into ways of hiding from God. Ashamed we may very well be, but, finally, what can we do, if we really want God, but come out from our hiding place, and stand, naked and defenceless, before him?

The question we have to ask is, do our pious practices, our spiritual exercises, strip us down before God, peeling off our masks and pretences, our false selves? Or is it rather that they are precisely the trees among which we hide, like Adam, hoping that God won't see us (cf. Genesis 3:10)? Whatever the answer, let us try not to deceive ourselves about this. If we are hiding from God—as we may well be, with at least part of ourselves—we should not pretend that we are seeking him; if our religion serves to protect us from God, then let us at least be honest about that, and even that little bit of honesty may wrest one of the devil's most cunning weapons from his grasp.

It is partly a matter of labels. We always like to have some label round our necks, some kind of definition of ourselves; perhaps it often seems necessary for our sanity. But we have to be extremely careful. Identity, in the last analysis, is something we shall only receive 'when we have overcome' (Apocalypse 2:17). Most people are now aware how much harm has been done in the church by the labels 'conservative' and 'progressive'. Used sensibly, they helped us to talk about certain realities in the church; but the more they became absolutised, the more pernicious and the less meaningful they became.

To define ourselves at all is almost inevitably to define ourselves against somebody else, and, before we know where we are, we end up judging everybody else. The Pharisees were undoubtedly among the finest Jews of their time; yet they almost inevitably slipped into the kind of prayer our Lord condemned. Genuine thanksgiving for the wonderful graces received in their movement of revival was almost bound to slip into condemnation of those outside.

For too long we have treated 'catholic' as a defensive label, defined against everybody else. It is painful, for instance, and at times comic, to read the Fathers of Trent arguing about the sacrament of the sick. They seem to have almost no idea of what they themselves believe about it; but they are absolutely certain that Luther must be wrong.[130]

Hasn't this for too long been the order of the day in Roman Catholicism? Instead of being the proclamation of the whole gospel of Jesus Christ, single and entire, it has been, for too many of us, chiefly a bastion against Protestantism.

At last the Vatican Council, especially in its Decree on Ecumenism, has tried to reclaim the word 'catholic'. We are no longer to see ourselves simply as a sect, defined against other sects. We are those to whom Christ's own prayer for unity has been entrusted, we are the seed of that unity.[131] We need to learn from all our separated brethren, precisely that our own wholeness may become more apparent.[132] If we take this seriously, the church has committed herself to rediscovering her own simplicity, so that all the things that go to make up her life (popes and sacraments and saints and indulgences, the lot) must be seen from the single vantage point of the gospel proclamation, the kerygma.

If this is to be realised, we must surely be very hesitant about adopting other labels. Marxism, Zen, Transcendental Meditation, Pentecostalism, all sorts of things may help us on our way, as we seek to enter into our inheritance of wholeness; but each one must become transparent to the reality of Jesus Christ, in whom are 'all the treasures of wisdom' (Colossians 2:3). We must not get stuck at the stage of preaching, let alone defending, any 'movement': we must pass straight on to the totality of the gospel.

We are pledged to simplicity, but not to a simplicity won at the expense of completeness. Our catholic tradition is committed to universality, universality of human experience, and universality of appeal, to men of all times and all nations. All the fragments of our experience, all the fragments of our world, are to be gathered into God's wholeness. That is the mission of the church.

It is not enough, then, simply to annex spiritual practices or doctrines on to the end of an otherwise unaffected catholicism. In view of the fragmentation of recent catholicism this is, I repeat, a serious temptation, which is easily not even noticed as such, especially in a situation as exciting as the meeting with Pentecostalism.

What we must seek to do is to learn from everyone the treasures, the graces, that are theirs, confident that, in some way, they already have their appointed place in the wholeness given in trust to the church. We need to learn from other christians, as the Council taught, to further the full manifestation of our own catholicity. If our catholicism means anything at all, then this is the most comprehensive 'label' of all for us to work under, the most comprehensive vision of all to aspire to.

Whatever we learn, whatever practices we adopt, then, from Pentecostalism (or anyone else) must be situated in terms of our own tradition, so as to challenge us as to our fidelity to that tradition, as to our grasp of its wholeness and completeness. And we must let ourselves be shattered in any such encounter; prone as we always are to reducing the gospel to an ideology or a movement, we need to be constantly shaken up in this way. Here we have no abiding city, and all our theological, ecclesiological and spiritual syntheses can be no more than provisional.

We should avoid making a 'thing' out of any new development, we should not seek to consolidate a 'movement'. We must allow God's Spirit to keep us moving, accepting gratefully all that he gives us, from whatever quarter. And so, please God, he will lead us into all truth, into the full knowledge of all that was given to us, once and for all, in the man Jesus Christ.

CHAPTER TWELVE

MYSTICISM AND MAGIC

OURS IS AN AGE of great spiritual revival; mysticism in all its forms is 'in'. And it is interesting to notice how united its voice is, from Zen Buddhism to Pentecostalism. Pentecostalism and Zen both bid us 'let go' (though Pentecostals add 'and let God'). Pentecostalism curiously echoes the early monks in its yearning for 'purity of heart'. Occultists, devotees of the Chinese *I Ching* (Book of Changes) and Pentecostals all bid us seek for guidance from some more than human, more than rational, source (as did St Ignatius of Loyola, though that bit of his Exercises is all too often forgotten). Hindus and LSD-trippers and Pentecostals all speak of extra-sensory adventures and exploits with the same seriousness. Spiritualists, magicians, and Pentecostals all revel in spiritual healing, often with the aid of what they all call 'creative imagination'. Watchman Nee, that remarkable Chinese christian, is as keen as any Buddhist or Taoist to free us from our ego.

What we must recognise is that—as mystics of all religions have taught, explicitly or implicitly—the way to the spiritual lies through the psychic. And it is not simply that we must pass through psychic phenomena on the way to spiritual phenomena; there may be no *phenomenological* difference between the two. The difference lies in the *significance* of the phenomena.

What is involved in all movements of mystical renewal, in whatever century or whatever religion, is a rediscovery of certain fundamental laws of the human soul, that get forgotten when too much stress has been placed on material things, or on intellectual and moral values. It has recently been suggested that psychoanalysis is an, admittedly limited, venture into mysticism, that it is, in fact, our modern, inadequate, version of shamanism.[133] It is certain that Jung was drawn into mysticism, especially that of the eastern religions. And oriental gurus have never been in such demand as now.

It seems that there are laws of the spiritual life which can be discovered and mapped out, more or less independently of religious considerations. Thus the church, east and west, has continued to derive immense spiritual benefit from the teaching of Evagrius of Pontus, even though he was, doctrinally, one of the most outrageous heretics that ever lived. And Abbot Chapman mentions that he used not to like St John of the Cross, because he was too 'Buddhist';[134] he later came round to admire him very much, recognising that the laws of mysticism are common to all religions.

Mysticism is, in fact, a part of our nature, and as such is an essential part of our renewed life in Christ. It is no more important than our minds or our bodies or our emotions; but it is, perhaps, the part that is most likely to get lost, at least in a civilisation as rationalistic and legalistic as that bequeathed to us by the Romans. It is therefore perhaps likely to appear more frequently in movements of renewal in the church, renewal being likely to occur precisely in those areas which have been most neglected.

It is perfectly natural that, in revolt against the aridity of mere dogma and legalism, strong appeal should be made, as by Pentecostalism, to *experience*. If God is real, this should affect our experience, as well as our understanding and our morals. But we must not confine him to our experience. It is his reality that ultimately matters, more than any of our doctrines or laws or experiences. 'We give you thanks *for your great glory*.'

So we should not be afraid of mysticism; only we must beware of its dangers, and not let ourselves be bewitched by it.

Perhaps the chief danger is that of spiritual legalism. Bruner has accused the Pentecostals of invalidating their profession of 'justification by faith', by turning faith itself into a work;[135] I think there is some truth in this. There is a tendency in much Pentecostal writing to lay down strict conditions for experiencing the Spirit at work; they sometimes sound surprisingly like spiritualists or theosophists. One finds this in Watchman Nee[136] and in that great American neo-Pentecostal Agnes Sandford.[137]

Now, it is quite true that there are spiritual laws, and it is often useful to know what they are. Thousands of people have been helped by the writings of people like Watchman Nee and Mrs Sandford. But this must not be confused with the gospel. In Christ, God gives us his Spirit without condition. God is not bound by the laws of our spirit, he is their master. In spiritual, just as in moral, matters we must see that there is a deep and joyful interplay between law and grace, our nature and God's free gift. God's giving does not depend on, or necessarily even wait for, our own effort. Although it certainly requires in us some corresponding capacity to receive, God can, if he wills, bestow the capacity at the same time as the gift.[138]

An illustration may make this clearer. God wants us to be humble. If we do not want to be humble, even if God gives us humility, we cannot hold it.[139] Our desire and God's gift must coincide. But if we desire humility, we cannot help but strive for it, and employ any means we know, to be humble. Our effort is, as it were, the symptom of our readiness to receive God's gift.

But, on the other hand, God's gift may come first, precisely to give us a taste for something he wants us to have, to create the desire for it in us. We then have to live into it, often by way of an apparent or even real falling off, before God can really give it to us and make it fully ours. This pattern applies in all his dealings with us, spiritual as well as moral.

God gives us his Spirit precisely to stir us to seek his Spirit. It is thus extremely important to be aware of the genuine principle of the charisms: they are given beyond the measure of our own sanctification, and one—not always the most important—purpose of this, is to make it possible for us to grow, to reach out 'above ourselves'.

We need to know the laws of the spiritual life, then, so that we can cope with what befalls, and see the hazards, and identify the blockages and problems we encounter, and become conscious of the things that hold us back. But we must beware of spiritual legalism, either in the form of binding God to the laws of the human spirit, or in the form of binding men to the fulfilment of such laws in order to be pleasing to him. It is not for us to lay heavy burdens on men's backs, when God's design is that we should receive the Spirit and manifest his works *by faith*. Works, however spiritual, however impressive, avail for nothing without faith.

The other chief danger is that we opt for some kind of magic, instead of true religion; and Pentecostalism, with its concern for 'power', is especially vulnerable.

Miraculous, charismatic works are paranormal, but natural psychic phenomena, inspired by the Spirit of God, and so integrated into the mystery of Christ. But the same phenomena, as such, can be produced by spiritualists and magicians as well as devotees of other religions. What makes them christian is their context and their significance. 'Many will say in that day, "Lord, Lord, did we not prophesy in your name, and in your name cast out demons, and in your name work many wonders?" And then I will confess to them "I never knew you; depart from me, workers of iniquity" ' (Matthew 7:22f).

Miraculous, prophetic phenomena, even if produced 'in the name of Christ', are no guarantee of salvation. This is a hard saying for our success-minded generation, which almost automatically assumes that 'if it works, it'll do'. Unfortunately, however well it works, it may not do. The Antichrist will work miracles as well as the christians, and, according to a legend of the eastern church (see Soloviev's *Tale of the Antichrist*), he will be a most successful churchman and leader of revival and reunion.[140]

It is so hard for us to see this straight, that the point needs to be laboured. We must escape from our materialistic prejudices, and accept once and for all that there is such a thing as magic, and it works. And it does not prove a thing.

There is a tendency in some revivalist circles to overlook this vital point. The gospel is preached in such a way as to suggest that its purpose is to bring us success in the world, solving all our problems and even making our business prosper. Jesus came, declares an American priest, to make us 'happy, holy and healthy'.[141] People cast care to the winds, and live entirely 'by faith', and everything falls into their laps; they get 'guidance' to plan their lives in every detail, and 'prophecies' to encourage them. It works wonderfully, and they are sure that

this is a sign of the Lord's favour and approval of their
'mission'.

Unfortunately, many a competent occultist can claim just
the same.

If we open ourselves to the Lord, for instance in a conversion
experience, or in receiving the gift of tongues, we enter into the
psychic field. If we are simply concerned to serve the Lord, in
all humility and trust, there is no particular need to advert to
this fact. It will look after itself. But it is true, for all that.

And if we are too concerned with success, it means that we
are now capable, or may be capable, of working elementary
magic. It makes no odds that we always do it in the form of
prayer in the name of Jesus; so do many occultists. There is a
spiritual law that if you are determined enough, you will get
what you want. Your 'prayer will be answered', but it may be
very little to do with God.

'If a wrathful man raises someone from the dead, he is still
not acceptable to God' (abba Agathon).[142]

Right in the middle of St Paul's treatment of the charisms in
I Corinthians 12–14 comes his discussion of love. It is only love
that makes our miracles acceptable in the sight of the Lord, and
love 'is long-suffering and kind, it is not jealous, or vain or con-
ceited, it is not rude or self-seeking, it has no bitterness, and
does not weigh up its wrongs, it takes no pleasure in wicked-
ness, but delights in truth; it is always ready to excuse, to
believe, to hope, to endure' (13:4–7). And the model of love
which is proposed to us, is our Lord himself, laying down his life
for his friends (John 15:12f).

'Death is at work in us, and life in you,' is one of St Paul's—
slightly ironical?—formulae for the apostolate (II Corinthians
4:12). He has to insist warmly to the Corinthians, fascinated as
they are by blatant spiritual prowess, that 'strength is made
perfect in weakness' (II Corinthians 12:9). The way of the
cross is what the bible offers us, and it is not a way of success. It
is physical, human suffering, that transforms our motivation
from human desires to the will of God (I Peter 4:1–2), so bringing to effect the grace of baptism. Jews seek signs, and Greeks
seek wisdom (and, in the context, this probably means mystical rather than intellectual wisdom), but we preach Christ,

and him crucified (I Corinthians 1:22f). We may be full of
spiritual gifts, like the Corinthians, and still be quite unspiritual
(I Corinthians 3:1).

There is a mysticism, and there are miracles, which are
worldly and serve the 'Prince of this world'. Our Lord Jesus
Christ did not come to make us comfortable in this world, he
did not come to bring peace, but a sword. His kingdom, to
which he has called us, is not of this world. He did not abolish
disease, and he warned us that the poor would be always with
us. He did not come to turn the oppressed, the underlings, into
prosperous tycoons; he declared them blessed, 'for they shall
inherit the earth' (Matthew 5:5). He sent us, indeed, to feed
the poor and to heal the sick, but we are not to think we shall
achieve this before his coming again (Matthew 10:23). Such
success as we now have is but a sign, a foretaste, of the fullness
of his kingdom. We are given no excuse for complacency about
all the injustice and suffering in the world; but we are bidden to
share it, and transform it in the name of him who had nowhere
to lay his head, and died an outcast 'outside the camp' (Hebrews
13:12f), so that when he comes again, all may rule with him in
peace. We are not only to cheer and comfort and heal those
who weep, but also to weep with them. Our Lord himself, in
the garden of Gethsemane, said 'my soul (*psyche*) is disturbed'
(John 12:27). He came, not in the superiority of power, but in
the weakness of love.

There is a power in the gospel, and we are commanded to
exercise it. But this power is made perfect in weakness, and if
we would be powerful for the Lord, and not just for success in
the world, we must take our stand on the weakness of the cross,
and on that poverty of spirit which the Lord himself declared
to be blessed.

We should be very wary of any spirituality that stresses too
much that we 'can do all through him who strengthens' us. If
we actually look this text up, we find that St Paul means something quite different from what some evangelists of the 'Victory'
gospel mean by it. 'I know how to be down-trodden', says St
Paul, 'and how to abound; I've been initiated into every kind
of circumstance: being full, being hungry, being well-off, being
in need. All things I can do (or perhaps, *bear*; the Greek liter-

ally just says "I can all") in him who strengthens me' (Philippians 4:12f).

This is the true power of the gospel, the power of complete trust in Jesus Christ, whether we succeed or fail, physically, mentally, morally or spiritually; the power of complete detachment from all phenomena, pleasant or unpleasant, inward or outer. 'I prayed three times about this thing, that it would depart from me. And he said to me: "My grace is sufficient for you" ' (II Corinthians 12:8f). Amen.

CONCLUSION

IT WOULD BE A PITY to conclude on a note of depression. The Lord's grace *is* sufficient for us, and that is really all we need to know. *All* power is given to Jesus in heaven and on earth, and there is now no condemnation for us who are in Him; there is nothing that can separate us from the love of God which is in Christ Jesus.

The nub of any real spiritual renewal in the church is this utterly simple faith in Jesus, this childlike confidence that he is Lord and Christ. This faith enables us really to cast our cares on him, and not to be 'anxious about many things'. Only one thing is needful, and that one thing is already decisively and unfailingly accomplished in Jesus. So we do not need to be anxious.

What we must learn from the Pentecostals is that, if we do 'let go and let God', things happen. God's promises are true, and we could do worse than get out our bibles and see just what he has promised. And then believe it.

But we should not make a 'thing' out of this. We do not have to become 'Pentecostals', nor do we have to start a 'movement'. Wherever we are, whatever our condition in the Lord, we should start there, and try to give the Lord that bit more scope in our lives, scope to be real, to make himself known, to work in us and through us, to plan for us and guide and protect us. In each one of us there is something stirring, some door that the Lord is knocking at, be it big or small. We should pray that we will find this door, and open it; that we will discover the working of the Holy Spirit in us, renewing us in the image of Christ.

If we can join together with other christians in prayer, this will be an immense blessing to us, and will contribute wonderfully to the upbuilding of the whole church. A network of 'prayer cells', as Fr Caffarel of the *Équipe* calls them—and this need not in any way involve any human organisation—may prove the surest way of genuine renewal in the church.

And these need not be formal groups. What is most important is simply that as christians we should overcome our embarrassment about spiritual realities, and meet openly and frankly in the Lord, in the 'fellowship of the Holy Spirit', as people living in the presence of God.

It may often be helpful for there to be more formal prayer meetings too, meetings specifically planned and advertised (though even then they should be as unstructured, humanly speaking, as possible; a group may need a minimum of structure to make it possible to pray at all, e.g. people may need to know who is going to start and close the meeting, and what the signal for the end is, perhaps the *Glory be*. But such structure should be as little as possible).

These meetings can be useful in many ways. If it is known that there is a regular meeting, people often like to bring to it requests for special prayer for themselves, or their friends and other concerns. Again, it can provide an introduction, for some people, to prayer or to more deep prayer. The faith of the group, and their freedom in the Lord, can help the faith of the individual; people often find, sometimes to their own great surprise, that they discover a whole new depth and simplicity and joy in prayer, through praying in a group.

Prayer groups should never be exclusive or élitist, or feel themselves to be in any way 'special', nor should they behave in such a way as to suggest that somehow praying in a group is far 'better' or 'stronger' than 'other' kinds of prayer. There is only one kind of prayer, the prayer of the Spirit in us; all other prayer is either aspiring towards that, or falling away from it. It makes no essential difference whether one is alone, in church, or in a small group.

There should be no pressure on any one to join a prayer group, or recrimination against those who leave it. It is a good thing if people come as regularly as they can, and it is helpful to have at least a nucleus of regulars. But if people find that it does not suit them, they must be quite free to leave, nor should their action be taken to mean anything beyond itself. If people want to come only occasionally, provided it does not disrupt the group, they should not be prevented.

It is a good thing that people should know that they can request prayer for themselves, with or without laying on of hands, for their spiritual or other needs, and that there can be a powerful experience of 'discovery of the Spirit'. But groups should sedulously avoid developing any kind of pseudo-sacramental initiation. Dr J. Massingberd Ford has sounded a warning in America against the Catholic Pentecostal tendency to set up a 'catechumenate' for 'baptism in the Spirit'.[143] It must be clearly understood that the only requirement for participation is faith and, at least in desire, baptism.

At the meeting itself, again, there should be no pressure on anybody to behave in any particular way. Each one must be free to pray as is right for himself. If, as is often the case, most of the group begins rather inhibited about praying out loud, it is probably necessary to make a fairly deliberate effort to pray aloud; and it is a good thing that people should pray loud enough to be heard without effort. But no one should feel forced.

Rather than uniformity of behaviour, what should be fostered in the group is an ever-deepening mutual sensitivity and patience and love. And in all things people should learn to look, not at each other, but at the Lord. 'Look to him *and shine*' (Psalm 34:6—'be radiant', as the Grail translation puts it).

It is to be hoped that we shall see a general revival in the church of all the various ministries and offices listed by St Paul. For too long the priest has had to shoulder the lot, and he is most unlikely to be naturally or supernaturally equipped for it. He needs the prophets and healers, and those gifted with supernatural wisdom and knowledge. If all these charismatic ministries are revived, this will probably contribute more than anything else to the revival of the true charism of the priesthood, which will be freed from other burdens, to be itself.

In particular, it is to be hoped that we shall see a revival of prophecy—not in the secularised sense, but in the true sense. We need men and women who know God's will, and are not afraid to be sent out to speak it.

We may expect, I think, that tongues will appear more frequently in the church; and this should be encouraged (sensibly!). And those who receive the gift of tongues should press on to interpretation and prophecy, as St Paul directs. If this takes place on a large scale, it could be the most important development the church has seen for a very long time.

We need a church that is bold in the Spirit of God; let us have less of this fear, this timidity. The Lord has fought the good fight and he has overcome! Praise to our God! We need a church that is not anxious about many things, that knows the power of her Lord. We need a church that is not afraid of mystical and miraculous phenomena. An increasing number of people, especially young people, are experiencing such things, and they need help and guidance, which at present is hardly ever forthcoming from christian ministers. We need people prepared to exercise the authority given to us by Christ himself, authority over evil spirits and diseases. In these darkening days, we need all the divine resources available to us. We need discernment to see situations as they really are, spiritually, and we need to know how to fight, when the occasion arises. The devil is not dead, whatever they may say; much that passes for sickness or depression or mere human discord is really due to haunting or other forms of spiritual or demonic molestation. And such things are going to increase. We are given the authority to act in such situations, and we should use it. Even short of fully-fledged public exorcism, which the church prudently reserves to the discretion of the bishops, there is often need and opportunity for all the faithful to give battle in the Spirit. Private and unofficial exorcism in the name of Christ is within the competence of any christian, lay or clerical.[144] Already in 1902 Noldin, the Jesuit moral theologian, expressed the hope that 'the ministers of the church would more often use simple (i.e. non-public) exorcisms, remembering the word of God: "in my name they will cast out demons"'.[145]

And we need to realise, in all this, the true power of praise and thanksgiving. Praise is a weapon that God has established 'to destroy the enemy' (Psalm 8:3 LXX); conversely, one of the enemy's best ploys is to deaden the spirit of praise in God's people. True christian prayer is always prayer with praise and thanksgiving, this is the vessel in which the prayer of the saints is offered to God by the angels in heaven. Sometimes, I think, prayer gets stuck; there can be an almost physical oppression, resulting from prayer that is not prayed through in praise.

If this seems strange to us, it is in very large part because we have lost touch with our own tradition. Our saints have always been men and women who praised God and delighted in him, and were not afraid to do the most outlandish things for him. We have Padre Pio in our own day as an outstanding example. The saints are not a race apart, they were ordinary men and women who let Christ have his way. They are the normal christians, and we are all called to sanctity. We should, indeed, admire the saints, but we must also imitate them, according to our own condition; and that extends to their miracles as much as to their virtues. Our Lord assures us that 'anyone who believes in me, he too shall do the works that I do, and greater than these, because I go to the Father' (John 14:12).

Jesus *is* Lord and Christ, and his Lordship is attested in our lives by the 'greater works than these', whether they take the form of raising the dead, or just smiling with God's own love and the power of Christ's exaltation to one of his little ones on earth who is in distress. He *is* Lord, and God *will* have his glory. And in that we too will find blessing and release from our cares. 'All shall be well and all shall be well and all manner of thing shall be well',[146] not in this world, but at the end. And as we 'home' on this end, on the heavenly kingdom, the new creation, the age to come whose powers we have already tasted (Hebrews 6:4), we feed increasingly even now on the food of heaven, which is to do the will of God; we enjoy even now the fellowship of the saints and angels, we have even now the pledge of the Spirit, whose fullness we hope to receive in bliss unspeakable in heaven. Even now we know the first beginnings of our freedom as children of God, 'and if children, then also heirs, heirs of God and co-heirs with Christ, provided we suffer with him, that we may also be glorified with him' (Romans 8:17).

LAUS DEO

CONSOLATIONS AND
SPIRITUAL JOY

'GOD LOVING THE SOUL' (wrote Reginald Buckler, O.P. in a *Letter to a Religious*) 'and the soul loving God; God giving himself to the soul, and the soul giving itself to God; God abiding in the soul, and the soul abiding in God; God working in the soul, the soul working with God; God *enjoying* himself in the soul, the soul enjoying itself in God. All this is expressed in the one sweet word CARITAS.'

I wonder how many christians ever think of *enjoying* God? Yet this is one of the scriptural conditions laid down if we want our prayers to be heard: 'enjoy the Lord' (Psalm 37:4—the Hebrew uses a very sensuous and hedonistic word) 'and he will give you the desires of your heart.'

Arintero devotes Question I, article 6, of his *Cuestiones Místicas* to 'the importance and necessity of divine consolations', and refutes at length the all-too common doctrine that such consolations are neither to be expected nor welcomed. He quotes from the sixteenth-century Franciscan, Francisco de Osuna, 'let no one think he loves God, if he does not desire to enjoy him . . . let us seek the Lord together with his consolations, as the just do, and not divide him from his sweetness, however much the devil exhorts us to do so'.

St Catherine of Siena teaches that there is no way to attain to christian perfection except through delight in the Lord: 'this is the way, and all must pass through it who want to come to perfect love'.[147]

St Vincent Ferrer goes even further, and lists, among the perfections 'essential to those who serve God': 'eleventh, constantly to taste and to experience the divine sweetness' (*gustare et sentire divinum dulcorem continue*.[148]

The official prayer of the church often bids us seek the joy of the Lord. One of the old prayers for Prime said: 'in this hour of this day, Lord, may we be filled with your loving kindness, so that we may rejoice the whole day long, delighting in your praise'.[149]

'He prayed, he prayed, then from time to time he lifted his eyes heavenwards and he laughed' (an account given of the prayer of the Curé d'Ars).[150]

Of course, our delight in the Lord develops and matures; its emotional content may give way to something quieter and more austere. St Catherine would have us pass through the 'love of delight', and be weaned from spiritual cupboard-love, learning to trust God without any comfort or perceptible help. But this in turn should lead to a deeper, continual awareness of God's presence, and a deeper, unshakable delight in him for his own sake.

The first stage on our way is likely to be fairly dramatic, emotional and even physical. Arintero maintains that any soul which is faithful to the grace it receives will, sooner or later, amongst other phenomena of the prayer of the quiet, show signs of spiritual intoxication, 'perhaps not quite to the same extent as when the first disciples received the Holy Spirit, but at least enough to inspire certain kinds of "enthusiasm", not so contained, but that it will seem madness in the eyes of some'.[151] He mentions some forms this may take: 'shouts and groans and songs of praise and leaping about for joy'.[152]

Father Baker's description of his own 'second conversion' (in the course of which he clearly spoke in tongues) is worth quoting. He gives a long, curious account of how this conversion affected him in various parts of his body, starting from his feet. And this exercise 'that I said to have been in hands, arms, feet, and legs' was not 'altogether without motion; for at times the exercise was with much motion. For half a year together his (Baker refers to himself in the transparent disguise of his "scholar") evening's exercise (not his morning's) had those motions in them, and certain senseless aspirations were joined with these motions, and the motions were very strong and violent, but yet passed and were acted with great readiness and facility, and no manner of harm or peril by them to corporal health or strength. For their invitation and enablement began and proceeded from the spirit and not from the sensuality. . . . Our scholar living alone was and might be loud enough in his voice, uttering and venting forth his foresaid senseless aspirations, yet not so but that he was sometimes in peril to have been heard by others; and if he had been heard or seen he would doubtless have been adjudged for a man that were out of his wits. But they who live in communities do commonly want such commodity of privateness and therefore must refrain themselves from such mad-seeming exercises when they are in company or otherwise in peril to be heard or seen by others.'[153]

It appears that Father Baker did not always heed the advice he gives about refraining oneself when in company. Crossing the channel, one time, 'he attended to prayer the most part of the time he was at sea, and some times he used very loud aspirations, calling upon the name of Jesus; of which thing we admonished him and desired him to forbear it . . . though he made promises and purposes to amend, yet still he did sometimes forget himself'.[154]

St Catherine, too, was sometimes unable to contain herself. One day she 'wept so loudly during Mass that Fra Tommaso was afraid that she would disturb the priests who were saying the Mass and told her to try to stifle her sobs when she went up to the altar. Being a true daughter of obedience, Catherine went far away from the altar, and begged the Lord to grant her confessor a special illumination that would enable him to realise that there are some movements of the Spirit of God that cannot be repressed. Fra Tommaso records that what the virgin asked for was revealed to him so clearly that from that time onwards he never again had the courage to tell her anything.'[155]

We may recall that for some spiritual writers uncontrollable weeping is the privileged sign of the working of the Holy Spirit.

The old Missal contained a prayer for the gift of tears: 'Almighty and most merciful God, who once drew a spring of living water out of the rock for your thirsty people, draw tears of compunction out of our hard hearts, that we may be able to weep for our sins, and, by your mercy, obtain forgiveness for them.'

We should not think that such exuberant manifestations and

experiences of God's grace are only for an élite. 'I think the devil does a lot of harm in giving people a wrong idea of humility, to stop people who pray from making any progress. He makes us consider it pride to have big desires and to want to imitate the saints and to desire to be martyrs. He tells us or lets us understand that we who are sinners should admire what the saints do, but not imitate it' (St Teresa of Ávila).[156]

What is important, though, is that we should not try to *ape* these phenomena. It is possible by an effort of our own minds and imaginations to try to imitate the spiritual manifestations of others, but, as the *Cloud of Unknowing* warns us,[157] the result will be madness or devilry. 'If it is truly conceived, it is but a sudden stirring, and as it were unavised, speedily springing unto God as sparkle from coal.' That is to say, the true work comes as spontaneously as a flame from a piece of coal on the fire, and requires no planning or effort on our part. We should not be afraid of even violent physical manifestations (the whole house shook in Acts 4:31), but we must not attempt to produce them, or work ourselves up to them, nor should we hang on to them or try to retain or appropriate them when they occur.

Nor should we ascribe too much to the Holy Spirit. Any manifestation of the Holy Spirit in us, is strictly a manifestation of the interaction between him and us; at least some of the physical manifestations we have been considering are to be seen as signs precisely of the recalcitrance of our nature under the operation of grace. They are, in one sense, signs of the Holy Spirit at work, but, perhaps more accurately, we must also acknowledge that they are signs of our resistance.

To conclude: Arintero warns us that 'those who do not receive' contemplation and experiential knowledge of God 'and especially those who refuse to receive it or do not sincerely aspire towards it, we can be sure that neither are their works truly religious'.[158]

We are all to aspire to the heights of mystical union with God; and, as a first beginning, we must be prepared to lose our dignity for a while, and get drunk with the sweetness of the Lord.

RECEIVING THE HOLY SPIRIT

I HOPE I have already made it sufficiently clear why I think we should not talk about 'baptism in the Spirit'; but we must face squarely the charge that, without this term, we are left with a terminological vacuum.

Now, to some extent, I think that we should all benefit from being obliged to 'fast' from jargon. Some styles of conversation are unhelpful and unedifying. We should not go around saying things like 'I have received!', 'Have you received?', as John Wesley pointed out a long time ago. If we want to give our testimony, we should do so in plain language, simply saying what happened to us, without dressing it up in fancy language.[159]

For theological purposes, I have suggested two terms that I think we can borrow from the christian east: 'discovery of the Spirit' and 'manifestation of baptism'. But these will not meet all the requirements of preaching and ministry. I would like now to suggest just three passages from scripture which can come to our aid. I do not offer them with a view to creating new jargon; our language must remain flexible, so that the Lord can give us the right words for each situation. But they can suggest ways in which we may, on occasion, want to talk or to pray.

First, there is Romans 12:2, in which St Paul says 'be transformed by the renewing of your mind'. 'Mind' here means the whole personality, not just our intellectual apparatus. What some people want, or ought to want, from the Holy Spirit, is that he will transform them by the renewing of their whole personality. Although this does not happen overnight, and we should never allow anyone to think that it does, there can be a decisive and critical experience of renewal and transformation, either at the outset, or at important moments in our spiritual development. Here is one kind of talk that can be appropriate and helpful.

Then there is Ephesians 1:16ff, where St Paul prays that God will grant them a 'Spirit of wisdom and revelation' that 'the eyes of their heart may be opened'. This too can be a definite experience, although it is always also an ongoing process. We can on occasion pray for someone to receive a positive experience of having the eyes of their heart opened by a Spirit of wisdom and revelation, that they may begin to know God directly and personally in a new way.

Thirdly, there is II Timothy 1:6, where St Paul bids Timothy 'rekindle the gift (*charisma*) of God which is in you through the laying on of my hands; for God has not given us a spirit of cowardice but of strength and love and self-possession'. St Paul is presumably referring to Timothy's priestly ordination, but we can apply his language much more widely. The gift of God —and his gifts are 'without repentance'; God does not change his mind (Romans 11:29)—can grow cold in us, we give way to a spirit of cowardice (or 'timidity', as the RSV puts it), we act so as implicitly to deny the gift we have received from God. We must rekindle this gift, and begin once again to walk in strength and love and self-possession. In this sense we can be 'converted' anew, and have God's life renewed in us.

This does not exhaust all the possibilities, by any means, but it does suggest three ways in which we can talk to people, inciting them to prayer, and indeed praying with them, if they so desire.

APPENDIX THREE

GROUP PRAYER AND SPIRITUAL DIRECTION

IT IS CLEAR that any group has a profound effect on its members, an effect that is only marginally controlled by conscious, deliberate factors; and that this effect may be for good or for bad. There is therefore inevitably a certain formative influence at work in any spiritual group (and this is obviously not confined to prayer groups), and this raises a fundamental question, that we ought not to evade. Some people, impressed by the way in which a group can uplift and mature its members, may feel that here is an answer to the general lack of good spiritual directors today. Others, more impressed by the danger that a group will simply ensnare its members in that kind of complacency which settles so easily on a group, will feel that the whole enterprise of praying together is so hazardous as to be not even worth considering.

There should be no question, I hope, of a prayer group simply ousting individual spiritual direction, where this is available. The question that we do have to ask, I think, is to what extent and in what manner is it spiritually prudent to expose oneself to the influence of a group? To what extent and in what ways can one properly look to a group to fill the same kind of rôle that is otherwise, and perhaps more normatively, filled by individual spiritual direction?

The first thing to establish is precisely the significance of the spiritual-direction function in christianity.

All the major world religions agree on the importance of the *guru*, the spiritual teacher. 'Do-it-yourself' spirituality, however popular these days, is a modern and rather suspect invention. The *guru*, exercising some mysterious spiritual power,

is capable of 'initiating' disciples, giving them, sometimes by
means of physical contact (such as laying on of hands), a
spiritual experience to launch them or further them on their
way. This is well attested in ancient times, and is known today
in a variety of religions, and provides an obvious point of
contact with Pentecostal practice.

In christianity Jesus himself is the one Master, and he has
reserved to himself, for all time, the rôle of *guru* and spiritual
guide (Matthew 23:8). Christians are all anointed by the Holy
One himself, and do not need human instruction (I John 2:20
and 27); and this is not something accidental: it is one of the
distinguishing features of the messianic dispensation (Jeremiah 31:33-4). According to scholastic doctrine, the gifts of
the Spirit, including wisdom and knowledge and understanding, are given to all christians at baptism.

But this supernatural knowledge must be, as it were, acti-
vated. The classic distinction between human and divine
wisdom, is that the former can be acquired by anyone who is
prepared to put in the necessary hard work, but the latter can
only be obtained by those who are pure in heart.[160] The
realisation of the supernatural gift of wisdom is part of what
we have called the 'manifestation of baptism'.

And, just as the gift of the divine life in the first place is
mediated through human ministers (cf. Romans 10:14), who
may even be called fathers (I Corinthians 4:15—'and who is
your spiritual father? Surely, after God, the priest who baptised
you', as Amphilochius of Iconium says),[161] so the subsequent
unfolding of the gift of the Spirit also involves human teachers,
appointed by the Spirit (I Corinthians 12:28); St Paul can
even say that he is in travail a second time until Christ is
formed in the Galatian christians (Galatians 4:19).

Many of the things impeding the full manifestation of the
Spirit are hidden deep within our subconscious, in the form of
compulsive reaction-patterns so habitual to us that we can no
longer even feel them to be alien to us. In this situation we are,
as it were, blind to ourselves, and can do little to help ourselves.
As one of the Desert Fathers said, 'no one can help himself,
particularly while he is still harassed by passions'.[162] Accordingly, one function within the church was recognised to be the

prophetic service of 'bringing to light the hidden things of men for their benefit',[163] a job entrusted down the ages to innumerable holy men and women, like St Catherine of Siena,[164] to name but one.

On the other hand, there is nothing that even a prophet can do, unless a man is actually prepared to listen, and to do something about it himself. 'A brother said to abba Anthony, "Pray for me." The old man said to him, "Neither shall I have mercy on you, nor will God, unless you begin to make an effort yourself and pray to God".'[165] As the Macarian Homilies teach us, without this effort on our own part, even if God gives us the grace, we cannot hold it.[166]

There is therefore a sense in which we may talk, as St Gregory of Nyssa does, of us being our own fathers,[167] in that it is our own will that must be turned to God, enabling us really to let him in and make us his children.

St John of the Cross reminds directors most insistently that the principal 'director' is the Holy Spirit working in each soul individually;[168] ultimately, the onus is on the individual believer to co-operate with the Spirit.

What the human director should provide, is essentially an objective point of reference outside ourselves, prone as we always are to self-delusion. According to St John of the Cross, he is to represent the faith of the church, and, interestingly, natural reason.[169] And this is seen as an application of the principle 'where two or three are gathered together'. 'We must notice,' he says, 'that he did not say: where there is one by himself, there will I be, but at least two.' Elsewhere he says, 'the soul that is virtuous by itself' (he later added 'without a director') 'is like a coal burning by itself: rather than blazing up, it will go out'.[170]

In itself this obviously has far wider application than just spiritual direction. Part of the standard teaching on religious community life is that even a would-be hermit should live in community first, simply because the rough and tumble of living together will automatically tend to open his eyes to his own shortcomings, hang-ups, vices, and so on, and without this he could easily delude himself in false complacency.

It is undoubtedly true that having to cope with people and

situations that refuse to fit into our cosy private worlds can force an issue: either a drastic stepping up of the processes of delusion, or actually facing up to ourselves. And even the former is not necessarily wholly disastrous, in that it will involve a marked increase in anxiety, aggressiveness, and so on —what St Paul calls the works of the flesh (Galatians 5: 19ff)— and Origen is probably right in supposing that if you go far enough in this direction, it becomes so oppressive that there is eventually far stronger motivation for a total and radical conversion.[171]

However, groups are very good at developing little rituals of dishonesty, ways of systematically evading real issues. And this is as true of prayer groups as of any other, with the added hazard that playing the 'prayer game' can lull people into a comfortable assurance that they are being very spiritual, and do not need to ask more searching questions of themselves, and risk a genuine exposure to God.

There is something inevitably ambiguous about any kind of common life, as to whether people uplift each other, or drag each other down. The deciding factor, according to one of the Desert Fathers, is actually love:[172] the kind of love St Paul talks about in I Corinthians 13, which is not jealous or possessive, rejoices in truth (does not connive at self-deception) and not in sinfulness.

I think there are symptoms that can be discerned in a group that is likely to drag down rather than uplift. There will be, perhaps, too much concern to get people and keep people in the group; there will be a tendency towards ritualising its meetings, often going with an excess of planning beforehand. There may be a tendency to talk and act as if going through the performance of group prayer was *intrinsically* meritorious, rejoicing in the means rather than in the end. If there is a doctrine which suggests that this is *the* way to the experience of God, and that they have the *fullness* of the Spirit, then one is entitled to be very suspicious indeed. If there is a kind of anxious, busy quality, there is probably some skeleton hidden away in a cupboard.

Now this is not a simple black and white matter. People at different stages of their spiritual development need and benefit from very different kinds of assistance. What is freedom for one man, is a prison for another. St John of the Cross teaches that whenever God gives some communication to a man, he also gives him an 'inclination' towards the right person to share it with.[173] It is an important characteristic of the messianic age that it is now God himself who is our shepherd (Ezekiel 34:15; John 10:11ff, especially 10:28). So long as there is something going on, he will lead us, cajole us, bash us, into the right path. The only hopeless condition is that complacent tepidity which he can only spit out of his mouth (Apocalypse 3:16), that in-between state which is neither frankly fleshly nor authentically spiritual.

And this brings us back to what is surely the most fundamental thing of all. If all we want is to be left in peace and tepidity, then even if one were raised from the dead, we should not take any notice; but if we are, as far as we can, seeking to be more closely conformed to the likeness of Christ, then God is faithful, and will use even unworthy ministers to help and guide us.

It is better, of course, as the whole tradition says, that we should have a good director, who is experienced 'so that none of the enemy's contrivances escapes him'.[174] It is good, adds St Teresa of Ávila, that he should be a learned man—not, be it noticed, one of those timid, narrow-minded 'medio letrados', full of theories and devoid of wisdom, with which our modern society abounds; but a really learned man, with sufficiently wide and diverse knowledge to be open minded to the most extraordinary workings of God's grace. This kind of learning saves a man from falling victim to his own theories, and St Teresa even ascribes a charismatic quality to his teaching.[175]

But where these conditions are not met, it is still not a good thing for a man, spiritually, to be alone. 'If you are troubled by unclean thoughts, do not hide them, but tell them at once to your spiritual father. . . . If there is no one you have enough faith in to tell him your struggles, that shows you are not humble. To one who is humble, everyone appears holy and good. . . . Besides, if a man calls on God with all his heart, and then goes to consult someone about his thoughts, he will tell him what is necessary, or rather God will tell him by means of the human intermediary, even if he is unworthy and a sinner—after all, God opened the mouth of Balaam's ass.'[176]

This is a thought that recurs on the lips of the directors themselves. Abba Felix says, 'Now there is no word. When the brethren used to consult the elders, and then do what was said to them, God gave the words to be spoken; but now that they ask and do not do what is said to them, God has taken away the grace of the word from the elders.'[177] St Barsanuphius himself, the most famous director of antiquity, perhaps, says: 'I said nothing from myself, but I prayed, and then said whatever God gave me the confidence to say. Not that I am worthy; but, when the need arose, God opened even the ass's mouth.'[178]

This is surely what underlies the stories repeated so often by the monks of old, of men reaching the heights of sanctity under obedience to notoriously bad, even drunken, spiritual fathers. This is the faith that inspired the young Macarius, when he left his cell, saying to himself: 'Whoever you meet, ask him for help'—a faith that did not go unrewarded, as he found what he wanted on the lips of a young cowherd.[179]

The essential teaching is finely recapitulated by St Dorotheus of Gaza: 'indeed, if anyone really wants the will of God with all his heart, God never leaves him, but always leads him in every way according to his will. Indeed, if a man directs his heart towards the will of God, God enlightens even a little child to speak his will to him. But if anyone does not really want the will of God, even if he goes to a prophet, God puts into the prophet's heart an answer according to the man's own crooked heart. As the bible says: "If the prophet is deceived and speaks, it is I the Lord who have deceived him" (Ezekiel 14:9). Therefore we should direct ourselves with all our might towards the will of God, and put no trust in our own hearts.'[180]

So we need to be aware that there are dangerous men and dangerous groups, and, not least, that we ourselves may be profoundly dangerous to ourselves and to others. And then we must simply entrust ourselves to the guidance of God himself, in the fellowship of the whole church, and aware, so far as we can be, of her teaching and experience. We should try not to be intimidated by theory, but seek always to broaden and deepen our awareness of the greatness of God's operations. And then, without prejudice to these other factors, we must be prepared to notice and even to follow the deepest attractions and inclinations that we feel within us. For instance, if we feel cramped in a group, it is possible that we are in fact being cramped; and if we find in us no real sense of commitment to the group, no sense of belonging, then we should leave it, freely and without ill-will, as far as we are able. We may, on the other hand, find ourselves cramped, but nevertheless convinced, not rationally, but with all our being, that we belong there. In that case, we must be patient, not deceiving ourselves, trying not to be unforgiving, and see why God has kept us there.

In the last analysis, though there are external symptoms, there are no external criteria by which we can judge of these things. Symeon the New Theologian explicitly raises the question of how you should choose your spiritual father, and he can only answer, in effect, that it is by the Spirit that we discern spiritual men.[181] We must trust in the Spirit whom we have received, and let him lead us, trusting that where we feel confident to go, deeply confident, there is where he will teach us.

Cowards, we are told, will not inherit the kingdom (Apocalypse 21:8), so let us end on this note of confidence in God, with a text from John of St Thomas, a true son of St Dominic, who, we hear over and over again, 'trusted greatly in God';[182] John is commenting on St John 3:8, 'you do not know where it is coming from nor where it is going': 'here we are taught that we should not be troubled, if, in our works, it is not always clear of what spirit they are, especially in exalted and unusual works, because although the Spirit very frequently moves us inwardly, and prompts us and stirs us, yet we can never completely know where he is coming from or where he is going, that is to say his principle or goal, and so the Spirit of God eludes us. And there are many people who would like always to act with complete security and certainty, and they are often held back from these motions of the Holy Spirit, because of the narrowness of their hearts, and so they are not suitable to be moved to great or exalted works, until their heart is widened to have great confidence in God and in his inward assistance'.[183]

LAUDARE * BENEDICERE * PRAEDICARE

NOTES

1. Brother Lawrence, *The Practice of the Presence of God*, Letter 6. I quote from the English edition of 1824, currently published by Mowbrays.

2. *Decree on the Ministry and Life of Priests*, n. 2. ET, most conveniently, in *The Documents of Vatican II*, ed. Walter Abbott SJ (Geoffrey Chapman, 1966).

3. *Decree on Oecumenism*, n. 4. (See 2 above.)

4. Julian of Norwich, *Revelations of Divine Love*, ch. 41. There is a slightly modernised version by James Walshe SJ (Burns Oates, 1961).

5. Dom John Chapman, *Spiritual Letters*, ed. Roger Huddleston, 2nd ed. (Sheed and Ward, 1954); Editor's Preface, p. 25.

6. *Apophthegmata Patrum*, alphabetical collection, Sisoes 12.

7. St Catherine of Siena, *Dialogue*, ch. 133. There is an ET by Algar Thorold (London, 1896).

8. St Catherine of Siena, *Dialogue*, ch. 15. (See 7 above.)

9. St Thomas Aquinas, *Summa Theologiae* Ia IIae q. 65 art. 2; IIa IIae q. 23 art. 4.

10. Archbishop Anthony Bloom, *School for Prayer* (Darton, Longman and Todd, 1970), pp. xv.–xvi.

11. St Thomas Aquinas, *Summa Theologiae* Ia IIae q. 9 art. 6, q. 10 art. 4.

12. John of St Thomas, *Cursus Theologicus*, q. 70, disp. 18, art. 1, 5. There is a rather inadequate ET of this *disputatio*: *The Gifts of the Holy Ghost*, trans. Dominic Hughes (Sheed and Ward, 1951).

13. *Little Flowers of St Francis*, 15.

14. St Ignatius of Antioch, *to the Ephesians* 13, 1. ET in *Early Christian Writings*, trans. Maxwell Staniforth (Penguin Books).

15. St Justin Martyr, *First Apology* 67, 5. St Hippolytus, *Apostolic Tradition* 10.

16. St Thomas Aquinas, *Summa Theologiae* Ia IIae q. 106 art. 1.

17. St Thomas Aquinas, *Summa Theologiae* Ia IIae q. 68 art. 2.

18. *Contemplative Prayer* by Père de la Taille (Burns Oates, 1926).

19. St Catherine of Siena, *Dialogue*, ch. 63. (See 7 above.)

20. *Constitution on the Church* ch. 5. (See 2 above.)

21. St Cyril of Jerusalem, *Procatechesis* 17. There is a handy ET with Greek text, ed. F. L. Cross, *St Cyril of Jerusalem's Lectures on the Christian Sacraments* (S.P.C.K., 1951).

22. St Catherine of Siena, *Dialogue*, ch. 56. I quote from the fifteenth century ET, *The Orcherd of Syon*, ed. Phyllis Hodgson (Early English Text Society, 1966), p. 130.

23. On Pentecostalism, see Michael Harper, *As at the Beginning* (Hodder and Stoughton, 1965). On Catholic Pentecostalism, see: Kevin and Dorothy Ranaghan, *Catholic Pentecostais* (Paulist Press, 1969); Robert M. Balkam, *The Pentecostal Movement in the Catholic Church in the United States* (Clergy Review, March 1970); Edward D. O'Connor C.S.C., *The Pentecostal Movement in the Catholic Church* (Notre Dame, 1971; reviewed by the present writer in New Blackfriars, October 1971).

24. Leo XIII, *Divinum illud munus* (9 May, 1897), para. 17.

25. Cf. *New Catholic Encyclopaedia*, s.v. *Mysticism*, vo X, p. 176. See, for instance, Rég. Garrigou-Lagrange, *Les Trois Âges de la Vie Intérieure* (Paris 1938). ET: *Three Ages of the Interior Life*, trans. Timothea Doyle (Herder, 1947–9).

26. De La Taille: *op. cit.* (see 18 above).

27. A. Poulain, *Des Grâces d'Oraison* (Paris, 1901). ET: *The Graces of Interior Prayer*, trans. Leonora L. Yorke Smith (London, 1910).

28. Anselm Stolz, *Theologie der Mystik* (Regensburg, 1936). ET: *The Doctrine of Spiritual Perfection*, tr. Aidan Williams (Herder, 1938).

29. See, for instance, Bede Jarrett, *Meditations on the Holy Ghost* (C.T.S., taken from *Meditations for Layfolk*), and *The Abiding Presence of the Holy Ghost* (Burns Oates, 1934).

30. See, for instance, Gerald Vann, *The Divine Pity* (1945) and *The Water and the Fire* (1954).

31. J. G. Arintero, *La Evolución Mística* (1908). ET: *The Mystical Evolution in the Development and Vitality of the Church*, trans. Jordan Aumann (Herder, 1949). *Cuestiones Místicas* (1916). The last part of this appeared in ET as: *Stages in Prayer*, trans. Kathleen Pond (Blackfriars, 1957). For the points mentioned here, see especially *La Evol. Mist.* II 9, 1 and *Stages* pp. 68, 80ff.

32. Karl Rahner, *The Dynamic Element in the Church*, trans. W. J. O'Hara (Herder, 1964).

33. *Acta Apostolicae Sedis* 51 (1959), p. 832. ET in Abbott p. 793. (See 2 above.)

34. Vincent McNabb, *The Craft of Prayer* (Burns Oates, 1935).

35. O'Connor, *The Pentecostal Movement*, p. 241. (See 23 above.)

36. John Wesley, *Plain Account of Christian Perfection* (Epworth Press, 1952), p. 88

37. J. D. Dunn, *Baptism in the Holy Spirit* (SCM 1970).

38. Frederick Dale Bruner, *A Theology of the Holy Spirit* (Hodder and Stoughton, 1971).

39. St Justin Martyr, *Dialogue with Trypho* 88, 3; *Odes of Solomon* 24; *Sibylline Oracles* VI 3–7. Cf. J. Daniélou, *Theology of Jewish Christianity*, pp. 224ff.

40. St Thomas, *Summa Theclogiae*, III q. 76, art. 1 ad 1.

41. St Augustine, *On the Gospel of John* VI 7.

42. St Thomas, *Summa Theologiae* III q. 64 art. 1.

43. Nicholas Cabasilas, *Life in Christ* II (*Patrologia Graeca* 150, 537AC, 568C).

44. Jerome the Greek, *The Effect of Baptism* (*Patrologia Graeca* 40, 860–1).

45. St John of Ávila, *Audi filia*, ch. 1 and 2.

46. Fergus Kerr, *Ataraxy and Utopia* (New Blackfriars, vol. 50 (1969) p. 312).

47. *The Cloud of Unknowing*, ch. 45.

48. St Catherine, *Dialogue*, ch. 46; ch. 36; ch. 48. (See 7 above.)

49. St Cyril of Jerusalem, *Procatechesis* 4. (See 21 above.)

50. St Symeon the New Theologian. 8 volumes of his works are currently available with critical text, introduction, and French translation, in the series *Sources Chrétiennes*: Catecheses and Thanksgivings (3 vols); Theological and Ethical Treatises (2 vols); Hymns (2 vols); Theological chapters. There is a critical edition of the *Letter on Confession* in Karl Holl, *Enthusiasmus und Bussgewalt beim griechischen Mönchtum* (Leipzig, 1898). The reference here is to *Theol. Chapters* I 35–6, III 45.

51. Orders and confession: see the *Letter on Confession*. Eucharist: see, e.g., Hymns 2, 11–15.

52. Basile Krivochéine, Introduction to Catecheses vol. I, pp. 19ff, the chief sources being *Catechesis* 2, and the two Thanksgivings.

53. *On Confession*, pp. 114–15.

54. *Catechesis* 20, 161–182.

55. *Catechesis* 28, 119–30, 220–230.

56. *Ethical Treatises* II 7, 235ff.

57. *Catechesis*, 28, 115.

58. *Catechesis* 34, 235ff.

59. Isaac the Syrian, *On the hesychasts* (Treatise 15 in the Greek

edition of J. Spetsieris, 1895, recently reprinted in Athens, p. 54; Treatise 14 in the ET by A. J. Wensinck, *Mystic Treatises by Isaac of Nineveh translated from the Syriac* (Amsterdam, 1923), pp. 85–6).

60. Cf. Arintero, *Stages in Prayer* (see 31 above), p. 39.

61. Isaac the Syrian, *On Faith and Humility* (see 59 above). Greek ed. Treatise 19, pp. 67–9; ET, Treatise 17, p. 353.

62. *Little Flowers of St Francis* 32.

63. St Catherine, *Dialogue*, ch. 162. Middle English ET (see 22 above), p. 405.

64. St Gregory of Sinai, *On silence and prayer* 2.

65. St Mark the Hermit, *On those who think they can be justified by works*, 85.

66. Evagrius Ponticus, *Practicus*, Prol. 50. There is an excellent new critical edition of this important work, with introduction, French translation and commentary, ed. A. and C. Guillaumont, in *Sources Chrétiennes* (1971).

67. St Catherine, *Dialogue*, ch. 119. Middle English ET (see 22 above), p. 266.

68. St Gregory Palamas, *Triads on the Hesychasts* I 3, 16.

69. St Gregory of Sinai, *Texts on Commandments and Dogmas* 113.

70. St Cyril of Jerusalem, *Catechetical Lectures* 17, 37.

71. Karl Rahner, *Visions and Prophecies*, ET by Charles Henkey and Richard Strachan (Herder, 1963), p. 20.

72. Vincent McNabb, *The Craft of Prayer*, p. 10.

73. Cf. J. Jeremias, *New Testament Theology*, ET by John Bowden (SCM, 1971), vol. I, p. 190.

74. St Irenaeus, *Against Heresies*, IV 33, 7.

75. St Thomas, *Summa Theologiae* IIa IIae q. 45 art. 3.

76. St John of Ávila, *Audi filia*, ch. 2.

77. St Irenaeus, *Against Heresies* IV 20, 7.

78. St Athanasius, *Life of Anthony* 34. ET by Robert T. Meyer (Ancient Christian Writers, 1950).

79. Quoted in Kallistos and Ignatius, *Directions to Hesychasts* 16 (h).

80. Postcommunion prayer from the mass for Ember Friday in September. Cf. St Thomas, *Summa Theologiae* IIa IIae q. 83 art. 17.

81. *Apophthegmata Patrum*, Ephraim 2 (see 6 above).

82. *Nine Ways of Prayer of St Dominic*, 6.

83. Eithne Wilkins, *The Rose-Garden Game* (Gollancz, 1969), p. 196.

84. *The Confessions of Father Baker*, ed. Justin McCann (Burns Oates, 1922), pp. 101–2.

85. Margaret Trouncer, *Miser of Souls* (London, 1959), p. 201.

86. Eusebius, *History of the Church* V 16–17; Origen, *Against Celsus* VII 3; cf. St Thomas, *de Veritate* q. 12 art. 9.

87. R. D. Laing, *The Politics of Experience* (Penguin, 1967); Mary Barnes and Joseph Berke, *Two Accounts of a Journey through Madness* (MacGibbon and Kee, 1971).

88. *Apophthegmata Patrum*, Poemen 11 (see 6 above).

89. *Cloud of Unknowing*, ch. 32.

90. St Athanasius, *Life of Anthony* 40 (see 78 above).

91. Walter Hilton, *The Union of God with Man's Soul*, falsely ascribed to Rolle, publ. in *English Prose Treatises of Richard Rolle* (Early English Text Society, 1866), p. 17.

92. Henri Ghéon, *St Vincent Ferrer*, ET by F. J. Sheed (Sheed and and Ward, 1939), pp. 112ff.

93. See the old Matins lessons in the breviary for the feast of St Francis Xavier.

94. E.g. John L. Sherrill, *They Speak in Other Tongues* (Hodder and Stoughton, 1965), ch. 9.

95. Tertullian, *On Baptism* 20.

96. G. W. H. Lampe, *The Seal of the Spirit* (2nd ed., SPCK, 1967). J. G. Dunn, op. cit. (see 37 above).

97. *Decree on the Eastern Catholic Churches*, nn. 13–14; *Constitution on the Liturgy*, n. 71 (see 2 above).

98. Quoted, without reference, in R. Newton Flew, *The Idea of Perfection in Christian Theology* (Oxford, 1934), p. xiii.

99. St Catherine, *Dialogue*, ch. 7 (see 7 above).

100. *The Life of St Catherine*, by Father Fen, Part II, ch. 21.

101. Denzinger-Schönmetzer, 620.

102. Denzinger-Schönmetzer, 1717.

103. *Apophthegmata Patrum*, Elias 3 (see 6 above).

104. Bl. Jordan of Saxony, *On the Beginnings of the Order*, 103.

105. Bruner, op. cit., p. 114 (see 38 above).

106. O'Connor, op. cit., p. 244 (see 23 above).

107. Bruner, op. cit., p. 170 (see 38 above).

108. St Thomas, *Summa Theologiae* IIIa q. 66 art. 11.

109. St Catherine, *Dialogue*, ch. 75 (see 7 above).

110. Tertullian, *On Baptism* 1.

111. Bruner, op. cit., pp. 244, 284 (see 38 above).

112. St Basil, *On the Holy Spirit* 16, 38.

113. Arintero, *Stages in Prayer*, ch. 6, pp. 29–30 (see 31 above).

114. See especially *The Interior Castle*. For a brief summary, see Arintero, *Stages in Prayer*, ch. 5 (see 31 above).

115. St John of the Cross, *Ascent of Mount Carmel* II 13.

116. Evagrius Ponticus, *Practicus* 56 (see 66 above).

117. John Wesley, *Journal*, Jan. 8th, 1738.

118. John Wesley, *Plain Account*, pp. 91–2 (see 36 above).

119. Bruner, op. cit., pp. 92ff (see 38 above).

120. St Thomas, *de Veritate* q. 12, art. 5 ad 2.

121. J. Massingberd Ford, *Fly United—but not in too close Formation* (Spiritual Life, Spring 1971).

122. St Bernard, *2nd Sermon on St Andrew* 4.

123. John Wesley, *Plain Account*, p. 34 (see 36 above).

124. St Thomas, *Summa Theologiae* Ia IIae q. 106 art. 1.

125. Henri Brémond, *Les Pères du Désert* (1927) p. xlvi.

126. *First Greek Life of Pachomius*, ed. Halkin, 135.

127. *Apophthegmata Patrum*, Euprepius 1 (see 6 above).

128. See Paul Christophe, *Cassien et Césaire* (Paris, 1969), especially ch. 7.

129. St Thomas, *Summa Theologiae* Ia IIae q. 106 art. 2.

130. *Concilium Tridentinum*, ed. Freudenberger, vols 6 and 7.

131. *Constitution on the Church*, n. 9 (see 2 above).

132. *Decree on Oecumenism*, n. 4 (see 2 above).

133. I. M. Lewis, *Ecstatic Religion* (Penguin Books, 1971).

134. Dom John Chapman, *Spiritual Letters*, no. 93.

135. Bruner, op. cit., pp. 247ff (see 38 above).

136. His best book is *Release of the Spirit* (*Gospel Literature Service*, 1966).

137. I recommend *Healing Gifts of the Spirit* (Arthur James, 1966).

138. St Teresa of Ávila, *Life*, ch. 21; St Thomas, *de Veritate*, q. 12 art. 4.

139. Cf. *Macarian Homilies*, 19. ET by A. J. Manson (S.P.C.K., 1921).

140. Vladimir Soloviev, *Kurze Erzählung vom Antichrist*, German translation by Ludolf Müller. See also George Every, *Christian Mythology* (Hamlyn, 1970), pp. 46–9.

141. Robert de Grandis SSJ, *Healing and Catholics* (Private Circulation, 1971).

142. *Apophthegmata Patrum*, Agathon 19 (see 6 above).

143. J. Massingberd Ford, art. cit., pp. 13f (see 121 above).

144. Cf. D. M. Prümmer, *Manuale Theologiae Moralis*, II n. 463 (Fribourg, 1923).

145. H. Noldin, *De Sacramentis*, n. 54 note 3.

146. Julian of Norwich, ch. 27 (see 4 above).

147. St Catherine, *Dialogue*, ch. 63 (see 7 above).

148. St Vincent Ferrer, *Treatise on the Spiritual Life*, ch. 20 in the

Latin edition of Fages (Paris, 1909). Ch. 22 in the ET by Dominican nuns of California (Blackfriars, 1957).

149. From the Dominican Breviary.

150. M. Trouncer, p. 200 (see 85 above).

151. Arintero, *Stages in Prayer*, Conclusions 1 (see 31 above).

152. Arintero, *Stages in Prayer*, ch. 8 (see 31 above).

153. *Confessions of Father Baker*, pp. 101f (see 84 above).

154. Leander Pritchard, *Life and Writings of Father Baker*, 261 (Catholic Records Society, vol. 33).

155. Bl. Raymond of Capua, *Life of St Catherine of Siena*, Part II ch. 6. ET by George Lamb (London, 1960), from whom this quotation is taken.

156. St Teresa, *Life*, ch. 13, 4.

157. *Cloud of Unknowing*, ch. 4.

158. Arintero, *Cuestiones Místicas*, Preámbulo VI.

159. John Wesley, *Plain Account*, p. 96 (see 36 above).

160. E.g. Evagrius Ponticus, *Gnosticus* 147 (quoting from St Basil, allegedly); *Capita Gn.* IV 90.

161. *Adv. Exercitationem falsam* (G. Ficker, *Amphilochiana* I, Leipzig, 1906, p. 34, 1–3).

162. Evergetinos, I 20, 4.

163. Irenaeus, *adv. haer.* V 6, 1.

164. Raymond of Capua, *Life of St Catherine of Siena*, Pt. II, ch. 4 (see 155 above).

165. *Apophthegmata Patrum*, Anthony 16 (see 6 above).

166. Macarian Homilies, 19. (See 139 above.)

167. St Gregory of Nyssa, *in Ecclesiasten* 6, PG 44, 701.

168. St. John of the Cross, *Living Flame* III 46.

169. St John of the Cross, *Ascent of Mount Carmel* II 22, 9–11.

170. St John of the Cross, *Sayings of Light and Love*, 7.

171. Origen, *de Principiis* III 4, 3.

172. *Apophthegmata Patrum*, Ethiopic Collection 13, 16. (French translation in *Les Sentences des Pères du Désert*, by the monks of Solesmes, 1970.)

173. St John of the Cross, *Ascent of Mount Carmel* II 22, 9.

174. St Nilus, *de Monastica Exercitatione* 28, PG 79, 756.

175. St Teresa of Ávila, *Life* 13, 18; *Mansions* (*The Interior Castle*) V 1, 8.

176. *Apophthegmata Patrum*, Nau 592/50 (French translation in *Les Sentences*—see 172 above).

177. *Apophthegmata Patrum*, Felix 1 (see 6 above).

178. Barsanuphius, Letter 808.

179. *Apophthegmata Patrum*, Macarius S 1 (in Guy, *Recherches sur la Tradition Grecque des Apophthegmata Patrum*, Brussels, 1962, p. 54).

180. St Dorotheus of Gaza, *Instruction* V, 68. There is an edition with French translation in the series *Sources Chrétiennes*, ed. Regnault and de Préville, 1963.

181. Symeon the New Theologian, Letter 3 (unpublished). See Irénée Hausherr, SJ, *Direction Spirituelle en Orient Autrefois* (Rome, 1955), p. 183—my debt to this book will be obvious to those who have read it.

182. E.g. in the Canonisation Process at Bologna, 26.

183. John of St Thomas, *Cursus Theologicus*, q. 70, disp. 18, art. 1, 7 (see 12 above).

WHO'S WHO

AGATHON, ABBA
See DESERT FATHERS.

AMPHILOCHIUS, ST
Bishop of Iconium. Cousin of St Gregory of Nazianzus. *c.* 340–395.

ANTHONY, ST
See DESERT FATHERS.

ARINTERO, J. G.
Dominican theologian and spiritual director, who taught at Salamanca. 1860–1928. He is a candidate for beatification.

ATHANASIUS, ST
Patriarch of Alexandria. Doctor of the church. *c.* 296–373.

AUGUSTINE OF HIPPO, ST
Bishop of Hippo (in what is now Algeria). His autobiographical *Confessions* became a spiritual classic. Doctor of the church. 354–430.

BAKER, FATHER AUGUSTINE
English Benedictine monk and spiritual writer; his *Holy Wisdom* enjoyed long popularity. 1575–1641.

BARNABAS, LETTER OF
Probably early second century. Nothing to do with St Barnabas.

BARSANUPHIUS, ST
An Egyptian, who lived as a recluse in Gaza, communicating with his numerous disciples through an intermediary, in writings, many of which survive. Died *c.* 543.

BASIL, ST
Bishop of Caesarea. Doctor of the church. *c.* 330–379.

BENEDICT, ST
The father of western monasticism. *c.* 480–*c.* 550.
BUCKLER, REGINALD
English Dominican spiritual writer. 1840–1927.

CABASILAS, NICHOLAS
A distinguished Byzantine lay theologian. Died 1371.
CAESARIUS, ST
Archbishop of Arles. A preacher and moralist. *c.* 470–542.
CASSIAN, ST JOHN
The interpreter of eastern monasticism to the Latin west.
Having toured the monasteries of the east, he settled in
Marseilles. He was a friend of Pope Leo I, and one of the
chief opponents of St Augustine's doctrine of grace. *c.* 365–
c. 430. His sanctity, although not widely celebrated in the
west, is undoubted and has been officially recognised.
CATHERINE OF SIENA, ST
Dominican sister. 1347–1380. She was a great mystic, and
spiritual teacher. She played a major and amazing part in
the political and ecclesiastical affairs of the time; she was
called to preach before the consistory of cardinals. She was
declared a Doctor of the church in 1970.
CHAPMAN, ABBOT JOHN
English Benedictine, spiritual writer and scholar. 1865–
1933.
CHRYSOSTOM, ST JOHN
Patriarch of Constantinople. Doctor of the church. An
assiduous commentator of scripture. *c.* 347–407.
CLARE, ST
A friend of St Francis of Assisi, and foundress of the Franciscan nuns. 1194–1253. Her body lies uncorrupt at Assisi.
CLOUD OF UNKNOWING
A well-known, anonymous, fourteenth-century English
mystical treatise.
CURÉ D'ARS (ST JOHN MARY VIANNEY)
Unlettered parish priest in France, whose fame spread far
and wide, attracting penitents to his confessional from many
nations. 1786–1859. He once declared, his face shining, 'I
believe that the church in England will return to its ancient

splendour' (Lancelot Sheppard, *Portrait of a Parish Priest*, Burns Oates 1958, ch. 12).

CYRIL OF JERUSALEM, ST

Patriarch of Jerusalem. It was probably he who instituted the ceremonies of Holy Week. Doctor of the church. 315–386.

DENZINGER-SCHÖNMETZER

A textbook of official church teaching, first started in 1854, and still going through edition after edition.

DESERT FATHERS

In *c.* 269 St Anthony dropped out into the Egyptian desert, to fight demons and confront God in purity of heart. Before long there were 'monks' in their hundreds in various desert places in Egypt, Sinai, Palestine and elsewhere. This was the beginning of christian monasticism, and their experience and teaching laid the basis for the spiritual doctrine of christendom, east and west. Collections of Sayings of the Fathers (*Apophthegmata Patrum*) circulated widely in many different languages. There is a selection by Helen Waddell, in ET, published by Fontana books. The monks of Solesmes are producing a fairly complete series of French translations.

DOMINIC, ST

Born in the north of Spain in 1170, he became a Canon, and then founded the Order of Preachers in 1221. His successor as Master of the Order, bl. Jordan of Saxony, wrote a little book about 'The Beginnings of the Order'. Somebody also wrote a treatise on 'The Nine Ways of Prayer of St Dominic'.

DOROTHEUS OF GAZA, ST

Sixth century. Disciple and secretary of St Barsanuphius, and himself a great ascetical and spiritual writer, and far more widely known in western christendom than his master.

ELIAS, ABBA

See DESERT FATHERS.

EPHRAIM, ABBA

See DESERT FATHERS.

ESSENES

A Jewish sect round about the time of Christ, with ardent

eschatological expectations. It is believed that St John the Baptist may have had Essene connections.

EUPREPIUS, ABBA

See DESERT FATHERS.

EUSEBIUS

Bishop of Caesarea; he wrote the first church history. *c.* 260–*c.* 340.

EVAGRIUS OF PONTUS

One of the most brilliant of the Desert Fathers, who was for a while Cassian's mentor, and whose teaching has had an enormous influence on the spiritual doctrine of christendom. His theological and philosophical speculation led him into wild heresy, and was condemned by two general Councils of the church, but many of his spiritual writings continued to circulate freely, often under somebody else's name (generally St Nilus). 346–399.

EVERGETINOS, PAUL

Eighteenth-century Greek writer, who made an anthology of ascetic and spiritual texts, including many sayings of the Desert Fathers.

FELIX, ABBA

See DESERT FATHERS.

FEN, FATHER

See RAYMOND OF CAPUA.

FRANCIS OF ASSISI, ST

A favourite amongst saints. 1182–1226. *The Little Flowers of St Francis* is a collection of probably apocryphal tales about him and his early companions.

FRANCIS XAVIER, ST

Jesuit missionary to the east, and now patron saint of foreign missions. 1506–1552.

GREGORY OF NYSSA, ST

Bishop of Nyssa, brother of St Basil; one of the great Cappadocian theologians, and a Doctor of the church. *c.* 330–*c.* 395.

GREGORY PALAMAS, ST

The greatest of all Byzantine theologians, and defender of

the spiritual teaching of the monks against both conservative dogmatic formalism and progressive secular intellectualism. *c.* 1296–1359. He is one of the most important saints in the eastern Orthodox calendar.

GREGORY OF SINAI, ST
A Greek monastic spiritual writer. Died 1346. See also HESYCHASTS.

HESYCHASTS
So-called after the Greek spiritual teaching of *hesychia* (quiet). They were not quietists in the western sense. They taught prayer of the heart, using the Jesus Prayer. An excellent introduction is the Russian *The Way of a Pilgrim*, ET by R. M. French (S.P.C.K., 1930). Further material is available in three collections translated by E. Kadloubovsky and G. E. H. Palmer, publ. Faber and Faber: *Early Fathers from the Philokalia*, *Prayer of the Heart* (containing the major hesychast writers, like Gregory of Sinai, Kallistos and Ignatius, etc.), and *The Art of Prayer*.

HILTON, WALTER
A famous English mystic. Died 1396.

HIPPOLYTUS, ST
Major Roman theologian of his period. *c.* 170–*c.* 236. His *Apostolic Tradition* gives an account of contemporary liturgical practice.

HOLINESS MOVEMENT(S)
A variety of evangelical movements arising in the nineteenth century, closely linked with revivalism.

IGNATIUS OF ANTIOCH, ST
One of the early christian martyrs (*c.* 107), and author of some of the finest early christian writings (see note 14 above).

IGNATIUS OF LOYOLA, ST
Founder of the Jesuits, and author of the famous *Spiritual Exercises*, designed to lead ordinary christians to a direct experience of divine guidance. *c.* 1491–1556.

IRENAEUS, ST
Bishop of Lyons, and the first major post-biblical theologian of the church. *c.* 130–*c.* 200.

ISAAC THE SYRIAN
A Nestorian spiritual writer, widely read in orthodox circles. Died *c*. 700.

JEROME THE GREEK
Apparently a monk; nothing is known about him. His writings seem to have influenced St Symeon the New Theologian.

JOHN OF ÁVILA, ST
A Spanish spiritual writer and preacher. 1500–1569. He was canonised in 1970.

JOHN OF THE CROSS, ST
With St Teresa he founded the Carmelite reform. Doctor of the church. 1542–1591.

JOHN OF ST THOMAS
Spanish Dominican. He devoted himself to commenting and expounding the thought of St Thomas Aquinas. 1589–1644.

JULIAN OF NORWICH
A lady recluse; one of the most attractive of the English mystics. *c*. 1342–1413.

JUSTIN MARTYR, ST
The greatest of the early christian apologists. *c*. 100–*c*. 165.

KALLISTOS AND IGNATIUS
Fourteenth-century hesychastic spiritual writers. Kallistos was Patriarch of Constantinople. See also HESYCHASTS.

LAWRENCE, BROTHER
A Carmelite lay-brother, whose *Practice of the Presence of God* remains one of the most popular of all spiritual books. *c*. 1605–1691.

LEO XIII
Pope from 1878–1903.

MACARIUS, ST
See DESERT FATHERS.

MACARIAN HOMILIES
A book of fifty spiritual homilies, of uncertain date or provenance; it is one of the most inspiring of all works to

come down to us from the first centuries of christian monasticism. John Wesley was enthusiastic about it.

MARK THE HERMIT, ST

A Greek monastic writer and theologian, who profoundly influenced St Symeon the New Theologian and the hesychasts. Flourished *c.* 400.

MENDICANTS

The Orders of St Francis and St Dominic, founded in the thirteenth century, which were to rely on charity and the providence of God, rather than on material, financial security. They played a major part in the spiritual and charismatic revival of the time.

NILUS, ST

Founder and superior of a monastery near Ancyra; a moderate and prudent ascetic and spiritual director. Died 430.

NOLDIN, HIERONYMUS

Jesuit theologian, author of a widely used text book on moral theology. 1838–1922.

ORIGEN

A theologian and exegete, who left a deep impression on all subsequent theology, although some of his own teachings were later recognised as false. *c.* 185–*c.* 254.

OSUNA, FRANCISCO DE

A Spanish Franciscan mystic, whose works impressed St Teresa. Died *c.* 1540.

PACHOMIUS, ST

The founder of the first monastic *community* in Egypt, at the same time that the hermit way of life was spreading under the influence of St Anthony. His favourite disciple and successor was Theodore. *c.* 290–346.

PAVIA

A north Italian town, where a local council was held, to reaffirm various existing canons, chiefly, in 850.

PHILOKALIA

A great collection of Greek traditional monastic and spiritual writings, made in the eighteenth century by Nicodemus of the Holy Mountain, on Mount Athos. See also HESYCHASTS.

PIO, PADRE
A saintly Italian Capuchin Franciscan, renowned for numerous miracles. Died 1968.

POEMEN, ABBA
See DESERT FATHERS.

PRÜMMER, DOMINIC M.
Dominican theologian and psychologist, author of a widely used manual of moral theology. 1866–1931.

RAYMOND OF CAPUA, BL.
A Dominican, and for a time Master of the Order, he was prominent in the renewal of religious observance. He was especially intimate with St Catherine of Siena, and wrote her life. This life served as a basis for the expanded Life which was translated into English by a certain Father Fen in 1609; this delightful Life was reprinted in 1867, with an introduction by the then Provincial of the English Dominicans.

SCHOLASTICISM
This term should not simply be used as a term of abuse, as it sometimes is. It refers to the style of theology which developed in the theological schools of the later Middle Ages, and survived, in a degenerate form, as the 'official' theology of the Roman Catholic church until very recently. Its finest product is the Dominican, St Thomas Aquinas (*c.* 1225–1274), a great original and comprehensive theologian and visionary, the Doctor of the church *par excellence*, and a great man of prayer.

SIBYLLINE ORACLES
A motley collection of religious verses, mainly Jewish and Jewish Christian, spanning the late pre-christian and first four christian centuries.

SISOES, ABBA
See DESERT FATHERS.

SOLOMON, ODES OF
An exceptionally beautiful collection of early christian prophetic poetry, from the first or second century. There is an edition of the Syriac text, with introduction and ET, by J. Rendell Harris, 2nd edn. Cambridge, 1911.

SOLOVIEV, VLADIMIR
A Russian philosopher, writer and theologian. 1853–1900.

SPIRITUAL FRANCISCANS
Rigorist Franciscans, who under persecution from church authorities, adopted extreme positions and fell into schism and heresy in the thirteenth century.

STARTSI
Russian word for 'elders', used especially of the outcrop of charismatic spiritual directors in Russia in the nineteenth century. There is a well-known portrayal of a *staretz* in Dostoyevsky's *The Brothers Karamazov.*

SYMEON THE NEW THEOLOGIAN, ST
One of the greatest, if at times controversial, Byzantine mystics. 949–1022.

TERESA OF ÁVILA, ST
See also JOHN OF THE CROSS, with whom she established the Carmelite reform. She is one of the great teachers of prayer, and was declared a Doctor of the church in 1970.

TERTULLIAN
A major early Latin theologian; he came from Carthage. He ended his life in the Montanist heresy, but many of his writings are orthodox, and his influence on subsequent Latin theology was considerable. *c.* 160–*c.* 220.

THEODORE, ABBA
See PACHOMIUS.

THOMAS AQUINAS, ST
See SCHOLASTICISM.

TRENT, COUNCIL OF
The great church council of the counter-reformation; it contributed greatly to the much-needed reformation of the late medieval church, and by no means deserves the unthinking abuse which it sometimes receives today. It was held 1545–1563.

VINCENT FERRER, ST
Spanish Dominican, one of the most famous preachers of his day, a prophet and wonderworker, after some years of learned and successful teaching. His *Treatise on the Spiritual Life*

enjoyed something of the position now held by *The Imitation of Christ. c.* 1350–1419.

WESLEY, JOHN
An Anglican priest who, with his brother, Charles, led a wave of spiritual revival, insisting especially upon the doctrine of perfection, entire sanctification; the two brothers were the founders, unintentionally, of a new church, that of Methodism. 1703–1791.